# THE
# LARGER
# CATECHISM

THE BANNER OF TRUTH TRUST

# THE BANNER OF TRUTH TRUST

*Head Office*          *North America Office*
3 Murrayfield Road   610 Alexander Spring Road
Edinburgh, EH12 6EL        Carlisle, PA 17015
UK                      USA

banneroftruth.org

First published 1648

This Banner of Truth booklet edition first published in 2024

Copyright © The Banner of Truth Trust 2024

\*

ISBN
978 1 80040 416 8 (booklet)
978 1 80040 417 5 (Epub)

\*

Typeset in 9/11 pt Minion Pro
at The Banner of Truth Trust, Edinburgh

Printed in the US by
Versa Press Inc.
Peoria, IL

# INTRODUCTION

Historically, the *Shorter Catechism* has received much more attention than the *Larger*. A study of the latter will reveal, however, that it is, as W. Robert Godfrey has noted, a 'mine of fine gold theologically, historically, and spiritually.'[1]

Struggling to make progress, in January 1647 the committee of the Westminster Assembly charged with preparing a catechism decided to produce two catechisms instead of one. They found that it was 'very difficult… to dress up milk and meat both in one dish.' Whereas the *Shorter Catechism* was designed for beginners in the Christian faith, the *Larger* was intended, in George Gillespie's (one of the Scottish commissioners) words, 'for those of understanding,' that is, those who were more mature and further along in Christian experience. It is also likely that one of the chief purposes of the *Larger Catechism* was as a directory for ministers as they taught the word to their congregations each week.

The *Larger Catechism* remains a valuable aid in developing understanding of the Christian faith. It provides outstanding summaries of some of the central doctrines of Scripture, for example on the subjects of justification and sanctification. Some have argued that the *Larger Catechism* is actually superior to the *Westminster Confession of Faith* itself in some areas—Professor John Murray held this to be true for its statement on the Covenant of Grace (Q. 30-32), which he deemed to be a better exposition than that contained in Chapter VII, Section 3 of the *Confession*. The *Larger Catechism*'s treatment of the Ten Commandments has also been considered by some to be an outstanding introduction to Puritan ethical thought. The *Larger Catechism* also fully develops a doctrine of the church—a doctrine that was so central to Calvin's teaching. Whereas the *Shorter Catechism* could be said to deliberately focus

---

[1] This brief introduction summarizes some points made by W. Robert Godfrey in his chapter on the *Larger Catechism* contained in John L. Carson & David W. Hall (Eds.), *To Glorify and Enjoy God: A Commemoration of the 350th Anniversary of the Westminster Assembly* (Edinburgh: The Banner of Truth Trust, 1994), pp. 127-41. Readers are encouraged to consult this chapter in its entirety for a fuller introduction.

on individuals, the *Larger Catechism*'s focus is more on the Christian community. The *Larger Catechism* therefore has a vital and necessary supplement to offer to the *Shorter Catechism* on the doctrine of the church and the outward means of salvation.

The most important value of the *Larger Catechism* is that it is a full, balanced, edifying summary of the Christian faith. This document is a crucial part of the treasure bequeathed to us from the Westminster Assembly, and churches in the Reformed tradition impoverish themselves if they fail to use it.

Today churches face a greater educational task than they have done for several centuries. Doctrinal ignorance is widespread. Pastors and teachers are often looking for useful, effective study materials. In response to this need the church must reclaim its great educational resources from the past. The *Larger Catechism* is a neglected tool the church needs today to help believers develop a vital and balanced Christian life and faith.

# THE
# LARGER CATECHISM

### Question 1: What is the chief and highest end of man?

**Answer:** Man's chief and highest end is to glorify God,[1] and fully to enjoy him forever.[2]

[1] Rom. 11:36; 1 Cor. 10:31. [2] Psa. 73:24-28; John 17:21-23.

### Question 2: How doth it appear that there is a God?

**Answer:** The very light of nature in man, and the works of God, declare plainly that there is a God;[1] but his word and Spirit only do sufficiently and effectually reveal him unto men for their salvation.[2]

[1] Rom. 1:19-20; Psa. 19:1-3; Acts 17:28. [2] 1 Cor. 2:9-10; 2 Tim. 3:15-17; Isa. 59:21.

### Question 3: What is the word of God?

**Answer:** The Holy Scriptures of the Old and New Testaments are the word of God,[1] the only rule of faith and obedience.[2]

[1] 2 Tim. 3:16; 2 Pet. 1:19-21. [2] Eph. 2:20; Rev. 22:18-19; Isa. 8:20; Luke 16:29, 31; Gal. 1:8-9; 2 Tim. 3:15-16.

### Question 4: How doth it appear that the Scriptures are the word of God?

**Answer:** The Scriptures manifest themselves to be the word of God, by their majesty[1] and purity;[2] by the consent of all the parts,[3] and the scope of the whole, which is to give all glory to God;[4] by their light and power to convince and convert sinners, to comfort and build up believers unto salvation:[5] but the Spirit of God bearing witness by and with the Scriptures in the heart of man, is alone able fully to persuade it that they are the very word of God.[6]

[1] Hos. 8:12; 1 Cor. 2:6-7, 13; Psa. 119:18, 129. [2] Psa. 12:6; Psa. 119:140. [3] Acts 10:43; Acts 26:22. [4] Rom. 3:19, 27. [5] Acts 18:28; Heb. 4:12; James 1:18; Psa. 19:7-9; Acts 20:32. [6] John 16:13-14; 1 John 2:20, 27; John 20:31.

**Question 5: What do the Scriptures principally teach?**

**Answer:** The Scriptures principally teach, what man is to believe concerning God, and what duty God requires of man.[1]

[1] 2 Tim. 1:13.

## WHAT MAN OUGHT TO BELIEVE CONCERNING GOD

**Question 6: What do the Scriptures make known of God?**

**Answer:** The Scriptures make known what God is,[1] the persons in the Godhead,[2] his decrees,[3] and the execution of his decrees.[4]

[1] Heb. 11:6. [2] 1 John 5:7. [3] Acts 15:14-15, 18. [4] Acts 4:27-28.

**Question 7: What is God?**

**Answer:** God is a Spirit,[1] in and of himself infinite in being,[2] glory,[3] blessedness,[4] and perfection;[5] all-sufficient,[6] eternal,[7] unchangeable,[8] incomprehensible,[9] everywhere present,[10] almighty,[11] knowing all things,[12] most wise,[13] most holy,[14] most just,[15] most merciful and gracious, long-suffering, and abundant in goodness and truth.[16]

[1] John 4:24. [2] Exod. 3:14; Job 11:7-9. [3] Acts 7:2. [4] 1 Tim. 6:15. [5] Matt. 5:48. [6] Gen. 17:1. [7] Psa. 90:2. [8] Mal. 3:6; James 1:17. [9] 1 Kings 8:27. [10] Psa. 139:1-13. [11] Rev. 4:8. [12] Heb. 4:13; Psa. 147:5. [13] Rom. 16:27. [14] Isa. 6:3; Rev. 15:4. [15] Deut. 32:4. [16] Exod. 34:6.

**Question 8: Are there more Gods than one?**

**Answer:** There is but one only, the living and true God.[1]

[1] Deut. 6:4; 1 Cor. 8:4, 6; Jer. 10:10.

**Question 9: How many persons are there in the Godhead?**

**Answer:** There be three persons in the Godhead, the Father, the Son, and the Holy Ghost; and these three are one true, eternal God, the same in substance, equal in power and glory; although distinguished by their personal properties.[1]

[1] 1 John 5:7; Matt. 3:16-17; Matt. 28:19; 2 Cor. 13:14; John 10:30.

### Question 10: What are the personal properties of the three persons in the Godhead?

**Answer:** It is proper to the Father to beget the Son,[1] and to the Son to be begotten of the Father,[2] and to the Holy Ghost to proceed from the Father and the Son from all eternity.[3]

[1] Heb. 1:5-6, 8. [2] John 1:14, 18. [3] John 15:26; Gal. 4:6.

### Question 11: How doth it appear that the Son and the Holy Ghost are God equal with the Father?

**Answer:** The Scriptures manifest that the Son and the Holy Ghost are God equal with the Father, ascribing unto them such names,[1] attributes,[2] works,[3] and worship,[4] as are proper to God only.

[1] Isa. 6:3, 5, 8 compared with John 12:41 and with Acts 28:25; 1 John 5:20; Acts 5:3-4. [2] John 1:1; Isa. 9:6; John 2:24-25; 1 Cor. 2:10-11. [3] Col. 1:16; Gen. 1:2. [4] Matt. 28:19; 2 Cor. 13:14.

### Question 12: What are the decrees of God?

**Answer:** God's decrees are the wise, free, and holy acts of the counsel of his will,[1] whereby, from all eternity, he hath, for his own glory, unchangeably foreordained whatsoever comes to pass in time,[2] especially concerning angels and men.

[1] Eph. 1:11; Rom. 11:33; Rom. 9:14-15, 18. [2] Eph. 1:4, 11; Rom. 9:22-23; Psa. 33:11.

### Question 13: What hath God especially decreed concerning angels and men?

**Answer:** God, by an eternal and immutable decree, out of his mere love, for the praise of his glorious grace, to be manifested in due time, hath elected some angels to glory;[1] and in Christ hath chosen some men to eternal life, and the means thereof:[2] and also, according to his sovereign power, and the unsearchable counsel of his own will (whereby he extendeth or withholdeth favour as he pleaseth), hath passed by and foreordained the rest to dishonour and wrath, to be for their sin inflicted, to the praise of the glory of his justice.[3]

[1] 1 Tim. 5:21. [2] Eph. 1:4-6; 2 Thess. 2:13-14. [3] Rom. 9:17-18, 21-22; Matt. 11:25-26; 2 Tim. 2:20; Jude 4; 1 Pet. 2:8.

## Question 14: How doth God execute his decrees?

**Answer:** God executeth his decrees in the works of creation and providence, according to his infallible foreknowledge, and the free and immutable counsel of his own will.[1]

[1] Eph. 1:11.


## Question 15: What is the work of creation?

**Answer:** The work of creation is that wherein God did in the beginning, by the word of his power, make of nothing the world, and all things therein, for himself, within the space of six days, and all very good.[1]

[1] Gen. 1; Heb. 11:3; Prov. 16:4.


## Question 16: How did God create angels?

**Answer:** God created all the angels[1] spirits,[2] immortal,[3] holy,[4] excelling in knowledge,[5] mighty in power,[6] to execute his commandments, and to praise his name,[7] yet subject to change.[8]

[1] Col. 1:16. [2] Psa. 104:4. [3] Matt. 22:30. [4] Matt. 25:31. [5] 2 Sam. 14:17; Matt. 24:36. [6] 2 Thess. 1:7. [7] Psa. 103:20-21. [8] 2 Pet. 2:4.


## Question 17: How did God create man?

**Answer:** After God had made all other creatures, he created man male and female;[1] formed the body of the man of the dust of the ground,[2] and the woman of the rib of the man,[3] endued them with living, reasonable, and immortal souls;[4] made them after his own image,[5] in knowledge,[6] righteousness, and holiness;[7] having the law of God written in their hearts,[8] and power to fulfil it,[9] and dominion over the creatures;[10] yet subject to fall.[11]

[1] Gen. 1:27. [2] Gen. 2:7. [3] Gen. 2:22. [4] Gen. 2:7 compared with Job 35:11 and with Eccles. 12:7 and with Matt. 10:28 and with Luke 23:43. [5] Gen. 1:27. [6] Col. 3:10. [7] Eph. 4:24. [8] Rom. 2:14-15. [9] Eccles. 7:29. [10] Gen. 1:28. [11] Gen. 3:6; Eccles. 7:29.


## Question 18: What are God's works of providence?

**Answer:** God's works of providence are his most holy,[1] wise,[2] and powerful preserving[3] and governing[4] all his creatures; ordering them, and all their actions,[5] to his own glory.[6]

[1] Psa. 145:17. [2] Psa. 104:24; Isa. 28:29. [3] Heb. 1:3. [4] Psa. 103:19. [5] Matt. 10:29-31; Gen. 45:7. [6] Rom. 11:36; Isa. 63:14.

**Question 19: What is God's providence towards the angels?**

**Answer:** God by his providence permitted some of the angels, wilfully and irrecoverably, to fall into sin and damnation,[1] limiting and ordering that, and all their sins, to his own glory;[2] and established the rest in holiness and happiness;[3] employing them all,[4] at his pleasure, in the administrations of his power, mercy, and justice.[5]

[1] Jude 6; 2 Pet. 2:4; Heb. 2:16; John 8:44. [2] Job 1:12; Matt. 8:31. [3] 1 Tim. 5:21; Mark 8:38; Heb. 12:22. [4] Psa. 104:4. [5] 2 Kings 19:35; Heb. 1:14.

**Question 20: What was the providence of God toward man in the estate in which he was created?**

**Answer:** The providence of God toward man in the estate in which he was created, was the placing him in paradise, appointing him to dress it, giving him liberty to eat of the fruit of the earth;[1] putting the creatures under his dominion,[2] and ordaining marriage for his help;[3] affording him communion with himself;[4] instituting the Sabbath;[5] entering into a covenant of life with him, upon condition of personal, perfect, and perpetual obedience,[6] of which the tree of life was a pledge;[7] and forbidding to eat of the tree of knowledge of good and evil, upon the pain of death.[8]

[1] Gen. 2:8, 15-16. [2] Gen. 1:28. [3] Gen. 2:18. [4] Gen. 1:26-29; Gen. 3:8. [5] Gen. 2:3. [6] Gal. 3:12; Rom. 10:5. [7] Gen. 2:9. [8] Gen. 2:17.

**Question 21: Did man continue in that estate wherein God at first created him?**

**Answer:** Our first parents being left to the freedom of their own will, through the temptation of Satan, transgressed the commandment of God in eating the forbidden fruit; and thereby fell from the estate of innocency wherein they were created.[1]

[1] Gen. 3:6-8, 13; Eccles. 7:29; 2 Cor. 11:3.

**Question 22: Did all mankind fall in that first transgression?**

**Answer:** The covenant being made with Adam as a public person, not for himself only, but for his posterity, all mankind descending from him by ordinary generation,[1] sinned in him, and fell with him in that first transgression.[2]

[1] Acts 17:26. [2] Gen. 2:16-17 compared with Rom. 5:12-20 and with 1 Cor. 15:21-22.

**Question 23: Into what estate did the fall bring mankind?**

**Answer:** The fall brought mankind into an estate of sin and misery.[1]

[1] Rom. 5:12; Rom. 3:23.

**Question 24: What is sin?**

**Answer:** Sin is any want of conformity unto, or transgression of, any law of God, given as a rule to the reasonable creature.[1]

[1] 1 John 3:4; Gal. 3:10, 12.

**Question 25: Wherein consisteth the sinfulness of that estate whereinto man fell?**

**Answer:** The sinfulness of that estate whereinto man fell, consisteth in the guilt of Adam's first sin,[1] the want of that righteousness wherein he was created, and the corruption of his nature, whereby he is utterly indisposed, disabled, and made opposite unto all that is spiritually good, and wholly inclined to all evil, and that continually;[2] which is commonly called original sin, and from which do proceed all actual transgressions.[3]

[1] Rom. 5:12, 19. [2] Rom. 3:10-19; Eph. 2:1-3; Rom. 5:6; Rom. 8:7-8; Gen. 6:5.
[3] James 1:14-15; Matt. 15:19.

**Question 26: How is original sin conveyed from our first parents unto their posterity?**

**Answer:** Original sin is conveyed from our first parents unto their posterity by natural generation, so as all that proceed from them in that way are conceived and born in sin.[1]

[1] Psa. 51:5; Job 14:4; Job 15:14; John 3:6.

**Question 27: What misery did the fall bring upon mankind?**

**Answer:** The fall brought upon mankind the loss of communion with God,[1] his displeasure and curse; so as we are by nature children of wrath,[2] bond slaves to Satan,[3] and justly liable to all punishments in this world, and that which is to come.[4]

[1] Gen. 3:8, 10, 24. [2] Eph. 2:2-3. [3] 2 Tim. 2:26. [4] Gen. 2:17; Lam. 3:39; Rom. 6:23; Matt. 25:41, 46; Jude 7.

### Question 28: What are the punishments of sin in this world?

**Answer:** The punishments of sin in this world are either inward, as blindness of mind,[1] a reprobate sense,[2] strong delusions,[3] hardness of heart,[4] horror of conscience,[5] and vile affections;[6] or outward, as the curse of God upon the creatures for our sakes,[7] and all other evils that befall us in our bodies, names, estates, relations, and employments;[8] together with death itself.[9]

[1] Eph. 4:18. [2] Rom. 1:28. [3] 2 Thess. 2:11. [4] Rom. 2:5. [5] Isa. 33:14; Gen. 4:13; Matt. 27:4. [6] Rom. 1:26. [7] Gen. 3:17. [8] Deut. 28:15-68. [9] Rom. 6:21, 23.

### Question 29: What are the punishments of sin in the world to come?

**Answer:** The punishments of sin in the world to come, are everlasting separation from the comfortable presence of God, and most grievous torments in soul and body, without intermission, in hell-fire for ever.[1]

[1] 2 Thess. 1:9; Mark 9:43-44, 46, 48; Luke 16:24.

### Question 30: Doth God leave all mankind to perish in the estate of sin and misery?

**Answer:** God doth not leave all men to perish in the estate of sin and misery,[1] into which they fell by the breach of the first covenant, commonly called the Covenant of Works;[2] but of his mere love and mercy delivereth his elect out of it, and bringeth them into an estate of salvation by the second covenant, commonly called the Covenant of Grace.[3]

[1] 1 Thess. 5:9. [2] Gal. 3:10, 12. [3] Titus 3:4-7; Gal. 3:21; Rom. 3:20-22.

### Question 31: With whom was the covenant of grace made?

**Answer:** The covenant of grace was made with Christ as the second Adam, and in him with all the elect as his seed.[1]

[1] Gal. 3:16; Rom. 5:15-21; Isa. 53:10-11.

### Question 32: How is the grace of God manifested in the second covenant?

**Answer:** The grace of God is manifested in the second covenant, in that he freely provideth and offereth to sinners a Mediator,[1] and life and salvation by him;[2] and requiring faith as the condition to interest them in him,[3] promiseth and giveth his Holy Spirit[4] to all his elect, to work in them that faith,[5] with all other saving graces;[6] and to enable them unto all holy obedience,[7] as the evidence of the truth of their faith[8] and thankfulness to God,[9] and as the way which he hath appointed them to salvation.[10]

[1] Gen. 3:15; Isa. 42:6; John 6:27. [2] 1 John 5:11-12. [3] John 3:16; John 1:12. [4] Prov. 1:23. [5] 2 Cor. 4:13. [6] Gal. 5:22-23. [7] Ezek. 36:27. [8] James 2:18, 22. [9] 2 Cor. 5:14-15. [10] Eph. 2:10.

### Question 33: Was the covenant of grace always administered after one and the same manner?

**Answer:** The covenant of grace was not always administered after the same manner, but the administrations of it under the Old Testament were different from those under the New.[1]

[1] 2 Cor. 3:6-9.

### Question 34: How was the covenant of grace administered under the Old Testament?

**Answer:** The covenant of grace was administered under the Old Testament, by promises,[1] prophecies,[2] sacrifices,[3] circumcision,[4] the passover,[5] and other types and ordinances, which did all fore-signify Christ then to come, and were for that time sufficient to build up the elect in faith in the promised Messiah,[6] by whom they then had full remission of sin, and eternal salvation.[7]

[1] Rom. 15:8. [2] Acts 3:20, 24. [3] Heb. 10:1. [4] Rom. 4:11. [5] 1 Cor. 5:7. [6] Heb. 8-10; Heb. 11:13. [7] Gal. 3:7-9, 14.

### Question 35: How is the covenant of grace administered under the New Testament?

**Answer:** Under the New Testament, when Christ the substance was exhibited, the same covenant of grace was and still is to be administered in the preaching of the word,[1] and the administration of the sacraments of Baptism[2] and the Lord's Supper;[3] in which grace and salvation are held forth in more fullness, evidence, and efficacy, to all nations.[4]

[1] Mark 16:15. [2] Matt. 28:19-20. [3] 1 Cor. 11:23-25. [4] 2 Cor. 3:6-18; Heb. 8:6, 10-11; Matt. 28:19.

### Question 36: Who is the Mediator of the covenant of grace?

**Answer:** The only Mediator of the covenant of grace is the Lord Jesus

Christ,[1] who, being the eternal Son of God, of one substance and equal with the Father,[2] in the fullness of time became man,[3] and so was and continues to be God and man, in two entire distinct natures, and one person, for ever.[4]

[1] 1 Tim. 2:5. [2] John 1:1, 14; John 10:30; Phil. 2:6. [3] Gal. 4:4. [4] Luke 1:35; Rom. 9:5; Col. 2:9; Heb. 7:24-25.


### Question 37: How did Christ, being the Son of God, become man?

**Answer:** Christ the Son of God became man, by taking to himself a true body, and a reasonable soul,[1] being conceived by the power of the Holy Ghost in the womb of the Virgin Mary, of her substance, and born of her,[2] yet without sin.[3]

[1] John 1:14; Matt. 26:38. [2] Luke 1:27, 31, 35, 42; Gal. 4:4. [3] Heb. 4:15; Heb. 7:26.


### Question 38: Why was it requisite that the Mediator should be God?

**Answer:** It was requisite that the Mediator should be God, that he might sustain and keep the human nature from sinking under the infinite wrath of God, and the power of death;[1] give worth and efficacy to his sufferings, obedience, and intercession;[2] and to satisfy God's justice,[3] procure his favour,[4] purchase a peculiar people,[5] give his Spirit to them,[6] conquer all their enemies,[7] and bring them to everlasting salvation.[8]

[1] Acts 2:24-25; Rom. 1:4 compared with Rom. 4:25; Heb. 9:14. [2] Acts 20:28; Heb. 9:14; Heb. 7:25-28. [3] Rom. 3:24-26. [4] Eph. 1:6; Matt. 3:17. [5] Titus 2:13-14. [6] Gal. 4:6. [7] Luke 1:68-69, 71, 74. [8] Heb. 5:8-9; Heb. 9:11-15.


### Question 39: Why was it requisite that the Mediator should be man?

**Answer:** It was requisite that the Mediator should be man, that he might advance our nature,[1] perform obedience to the law,[2] suffer and make intercession for us in our nature,[3] have a fellow-feeling of our infirmities;[4] that we might receive the adoption of sons,[5] and have comfort and access with boldness unto the throne of grace.[6]

[1] Heb. 2:16. [2] Gal. 4:4. [3] Heb. 2:14; Heb. 7:24-25. [4] Heb. 4:15. [5] Gal. 4:5. [6] Heb. 4:16.


### Question 40: Why was it requisite that the Mediator should be God and man in one person?

**Answer:** It was requisite that the Mediator, who was to reconcile God and man, should himself be both God and man, and this in one person, that the proper works of each nature might be accepted of God for us,[1] and relied on by us, as the works of the whole person.[2]

[1] Matt. 1:21, 23; Matt. 3:17; Heb. 9:14. [2] 1 Pet. 2:6.

### Question 41: Why was our Mediator called Jesus?

**Answer:** Our Mediator was called Jesus, because he saveth his people from their sins.[1]

[1] Matt. 1:21.

### Question 42: Why was our Mediator called Christ?

**Answer:** Our Mediator was called Christ, because he was anointed with the Holy Ghost above measure;[1] and so set apart, and fully furnished with all authority and ability,[2] to execute the offices of prophet,[3] priest,[4] and king of his church,[5] in the estate both of his humiliation and exaltation.

[1] John 3:34; Psa. 45:7. [2] John 6:27; Matt. 28:18-20. [3] Acts 3:21-22; Luke 4:18, 21. [4] Heb. 5:5-7; Heb. 4:14-15. [5] Psa. 2:6; Matt. 21:5; Isa. 9:6-7; Phil. 2:8-11.

### Question 43: How doth Christ execute the office of a prophet?

**Answer:** Christ executeth the office of a prophet, in his revealing to the church,[1] in all ages, by his Spirit and word,[2] in divers ways of administration,[3] the whole will of God,[4] in all things concerning their edification and salvation.[5]

[1] John 1:18. [2] 1 Pet. 1:10-12. [3] Heb. 1:1-2. [4] John 15:15. [5] Acts 20:32; Eph. 4:11-13; John 20:31.

### Question 44: How doth Christ execute the office of a priest?

**Answer:** Christ executeth the office of a priest, in his once offering himself a sacrifice without spot to God,[1] to be a reconciliation for the sins of his people;[2] and in making continual intercession for them.[3]

[1] Heb. 9:14, 28. [2] Heb. 2:17. [3] Heb. 7:25.

### Question 45: How doth Christ execute the office of a king?

**Answer:** Christ executeth the office of a king, in calling out of the world a people to himself,[1] and giving them officers,[2] laws,[3] and censures, by which he visibly governs them;[4] in bestowing saving grace upon his elect,[5] rewarding their obedience,[6] and correcting them for their sins,[7] preserving and supporting them under all their temptations and sufferings,[8] restraining and overcoming all their enemies,[9] and powerfully ordering all things for his own glory,[10] and their good;[11] and also in taking vengeance on the rest, who know not God, and obey not the gospel.[12]

[1] Acts 15:14-16; Isa. 55:4-5; Gen. 49:10; Psa. 110:3. [2] Eph. 4:11-12; 1 Cor. 12:28. [3] Isa. 33:22. [4] Matt. 18:17-18; 1 Cor. 5:4-5. [5] Acts 5:31. [6] Rev. 22:12; Rev. 2:10. [7] Rev. 3:19. [8] Isa. 63:9. [9] 1 Cor. 15:25; Psa. 110. [10] Rom. 14:10-11. [11] Rom. 8:28. [12] 2 Thess. 1:8-9; Psa. 2:8-9.

## Question 46: What was the estate of Christ's humiliation?

**Answer:** The estate of Christ's humiliation was that low condition, wherein he for our sakes, emptying himself of his glory, took upon him the form of a servant, in his conception and birth, life, death, and after his death, until his resurrection.[1]

[1] Phil. 2:6-8; Luke 1:31; 2 Cor. 8:9; Acts 2:24.

## Question 47: How did Christ humble himself in his conception and birth?

**Answer:** Christ humbled himself in his conception and birth, in that, being from all eternity the Son of God, in the bosom of the Father, he was pleased in the fullness of time to become the son of man, made of a woman of low estate, and to be born of her; with divers circumstances of more than ordinary abasement.[1]

[1] John 1:14, 18; Gal. 4:4; Luke 2:7.

## Question 48: How did Christ humble himself in his life?

**Answer:** Christ humbled himself in his life, by subjecting himself to the law,[1] which he perfectly fulfilled;[2] and by conflicting with the indignities of the world,[3] temptations of Satan,[4] and infirmities in his flesh, whether common to the nature of man, or particularly accompanying that his low condition.[5]

[1] Gal. 4:4. [2] Matt. 5:17; Rom. 5:19. [3] Psa. 22:6; Heb. 12:2-3. [4] Matt. 4:1-12; Luke 4:13. [5] Heb. 2:17-18; Heb. 4:15; Isa. 52:13-14.

## Question 49: How did Christ humble himself in his death?

**Answer:** Christ humbled himself in his death, in that having been betrayed by Judas,[1] forsaken by his disciples,[2] scorned and rejected by the world,[3] condemned by Pilate, and tormented by his persecutors;[4] having also conflicted with the terrors of death, and the powers of darkness, felt and borne the weight of God's wrath,[5] he laid down his life an offering for sin,[6] enduring the painful, shameful, and cursed death of the cross.[7]

[1] Matt. 27:4. [2] Matt. 26:56. [3] Isa. 53:2-3. [4] Matt. 27:26-50; John 19:34. [5] Luke 22:44; Matt. 27:46. [6] Isa. 53:10. [7] Phil. 2:8; Heb. 12:2; Gal. 3:13.


**Question 50: Wherein consisted Christ's humiliation after his death?**

**Answer:** Christ's humiliation after his death consisted in his being buried,[1] and continuing in the state of the dead, and under the power of death till the third day;[2] which hath been otherwise expressed in these words, *He descended into hell.*

[1] 1 Cor. 15:3-4. [2] Psa. 16:10 compared with Acts 2:24-27, 31; Rom. 6:9; Matt. 12:40.


**Question 51: What was the estate of Christ's exaltation?**

**Answer:** The estate of Christ's exaltation comprehendeth his resurrection,[1] ascension,[2] sitting at the right hand of the Father,[3] and his coming again to judge the world.[4]

[1] 1 Cor. 15:4. [2] Mark 16:19. [3] Eph. 1:20. [4] Acts 1:11; Acts 17:31.


**Question 52: How was Christ exalted in his resurrection?**

**Answer:** Christ was exalted in his resurrection, in that, not having seen corruption in death (of which it was not possible for him to be held),[1] and having the very same body in which he suffered, with the essential properties thereof[2] (but without mortality, and other common infirmities belonging to this life), really united to his soul,[3] he rose again from the dead the third day by his own power;[4] whereby he declared himself to be the Son of God,[5] to have satisfied divine justice,[6] to have vanquished death, and him that had the power of it,[7] and to be Lord of quick and dead:[8] all which he did as a public person,[9] the head of his church,[10] for their justification,[11] quickening in grace,[12] support against enemies,[13] and to assure them of their resurrection from the dead at the last day.[14]

[1] Acts 2:24, 27. [2] Luke 24:39. [3] Rom. 6:9; Rev. 1:18. [4] John 10:18. [5] Rom. 1:4. [6] Rom. 8:34. [7] Heb. 2:14. [8] Rom. 14:9. [9] 1 Cor. 15:21-22. [10] Eph. 1:20-23; Col. 1:18. [11] Rom. 4:25. [12] Eph. 2:1, 5-6; Col. 2:12. [13] 1 Cor. 15:25-27. [14] 1 Cor. 15:20.

### Question 53: How was Christ exalted in his ascension?

**Answer:** Christ was exalted in his ascension, in that having after his resurrection often appeared unto and conversed with his apostles, speaking to them of the things pertaining to the kingdom of God,[1] and giving them commission to preach the gospel to all nations,[2] forty days after his resurrection, he, in our nature, and as our head,[3] triumphing over enemies,[4] visibly went up into the highest heavens, there to receive gifts for men,[5] to raise up our affections thither,[6] and to prepare a place for us,[7] where he himself is, and shall continue till his second coming at the end of the world.[8]

[1] Acts 1:2-3. [2] Matt. 28:19-20. [3] Heb. 6:20. [4] Eph. 4:8. [5] Acts 1:9-11; Eph. 4:10; Psa. 68:18. [6] Col. 3:1-2. [7] John 14:3. [8] Acts 3:21.

### Question 54: How is Christ exalted in his sitting at the right hand of God?

**Answer:** Christ is exalted in his sitting at the right hand of God, in that as God-man he is advanced to the highest favour with God the Father,[1] with all fullness of joy,[2] glory,[3] and power over all things in heaven and earth;[4] and does gather and defend his church, and subdue their enemies; furnisheth his ministers and people with gifts and graces,[5] and maketh intercession for them.[6]

[1] Phil. 2:9. [2] Acts 2:28 compared with Psa. 16:11. [3] John 17:5. [4] Eph. 1:22; 1 Pet. 3:22. [5] Eph. 4:10-12; Psa. 110. [6] Rom. 8:34.

### Question 55: How doth Christ make intercession?

**Answer:** Christ maketh intercession, by his appearing in our nature continually before the Father in heaven,[1] in the merit of his obedience and sacrifice on earth,[2] declaring his will to have it applied to all believers;[3] answering all accusations against them,[4] and procuring for them quiet of conscience, notwithstanding daily failings,[5] access with boldness to the throne of grace,[6] and acceptance of their persons[7] and services.[8]

[1] Heb. 9:12, 24. [2] Heb. 1:3. [3] John 3:16; John 17:9, 20, 24. [4] Rom. 8:33-34. [5] Rom. 5:1-2; 1 John 2:1-2. [6] Heb. 4:16. [7] Eph. 1:6. [8] 1 Pet. 2:5.

### Question 56: How is Christ to be exalted in his coming again to judge the world?

**Answer:** Christ is to be exalted in his coming again to judge the world, in that he, who was unjustly judged and condemned by wicked men,[1] shall come again at the last day in great power,[2] and in the full manifestation of his own glory, and of his Father's, with all his holy angels,[3] with a shout, with the voice of the archangel, and with the trumpet of God,[4] to judge the world in righteousness.[5]

[1] Acts 3:14-15. [2] Matt. 24:30. [3] Luke 9:26; Matt. 25:31. [4] 1 Thess. 4:16. [5] Acts 17:31.

### Question 57: What benefits hath Christ procured by his mediation?

**Answer:** Christ, by his mediation, hath procured redemption,[1] with all other benefits of the covenant of grace.[2]

[1] Heb. 9:12. [2] 2 Cor. 1:20.

### Question 58: How do we come to be made partakers of the benefits which Christ hath procured?

**Answer:** We are made partakers of the benefits which Christ hath procured, by the application of them unto us,[1] which is the work especially of God the Holy Ghost.[2]

[1] John 1:11-12. [2] Titus 3:5-6.

### Question 59: Who are made partakers of redemption through Christ?

**Answer:** Redemption is certainly applied, and effectually communicated, to all those for whom Christ hath purchased it;[1] who are in time by the Holy Ghost enabled to believe in Christ according to the gospel.[2]

[1] Eph. 1:13-14; John 6:37, 39; John 10:15-16. [2] Eph. 2:8; 2 Cor. 4:13.

### Question 60: Can they who have never heard the gospel, and so know not Jesus Christ, nor believe in him, be saved by their living according to the light of nature?

**Answer:** They who, having never heard the gospel,[1] know not Jesus Christ,[2] and believe not in him, cannot be saved,[3] be they never so diligent to frame their lives according to the light of nature,[4] or the laws of that religion which they profess;[5] neither is there salvation in any other, but in Christ alone,[6] who is the Saviour only of his body the church.[7]

[1] Rom. 10:14. [2] 2 Thess. 1:8-9; Eph. 2:12; John 1:10-12. [3] John 8:24; Mark 16:16. [4] 1 Cor. 1:20-24. [5] John 4:22; Rom. 9:31-32. Phil. 3:4-9. [6] Acts 4:12. [7] Eph. 5:23.

**Question 61: Are all they saved who hear the gospel, and live in the church?**

**Answer:** All that hear the gospel, and live in the visible church, are not saved; but they only who are true members of the church invisible.[1]

[1] John 12:38-40; Rom. 9:6; Matt. 22:14; Matt. 7:21; Rom. 11:7.


**Question 62: What is the visible church?**

**Answer:** The visible church is a society made up of all such as in all ages and places of the world do profess the true religion,[1] and of their children.[2]

[1] 1 Cor. 1:2; 1 Cor. 12:13; Rom. 15:9-12; Rev. 7:9; Psa. 2:8; Psa. 22:27-31; Psa. 45:17; Matt. 28:19-20; Isa. 59:21. [2] 1 Cor. 7:14; Acts 2:39; Rom. 11:16; Gen. 17:7.


**Question 63: What are the special privileges of the visible church?**

**Answer:** The visible church hath the privilege of being under God's special care and government;[1] of being protected and preserved in all ages, notwithstanding the opposition of all enemies;[2] and of enjoying the communion of saints, the ordinary means of salvation,[3] and offers of grace by Christ to all the members of it in the ministry of the gospel, testifying, that whosoever believes in him shall be saved,[4] and excluding none that will come unto him.[5]

[1] Isa. 4:5-6; 1 Tim. 4:10. [2] Psa. 115; Isa. 31:4-5; Zech. 12:2-4, 8-9. [3] Acts 2:39, 42. [4] Psa. 147:19-20; Rom. 9:4; Eph. 4:11-12; Mark 16:15-16; John 6:37.


**Question 64: What is the invisible church?**

**Answer:** The invisible church is the whole number of the elect, that have been, are, or shall be gathered into one under Christ the head.[1]

[1] Eph. 1:10, 22-23; John 10:16; John 11:52.


**Question 65: What special benefits do the members of the invisible church enjoy by Christ?**

**Answer:** The members of the invisible church by Christ enjoy union and communion with him in grace and glory.[1]

[1] John 17:21; Eph. 2:5-6; John 17:24.


**Question 66: What is that union which the elect have with Christ?**

**Answer:** The union which the elect have with Christ is the work of God's grace,[1] whereby they are spiritually and mystically, yet really and inseparably, joined to Christ as their head and husband;[2] which is done in their effectual calling.[3]

[1] Eph. 1:22; Eph. 2:6-8. [2] 1 Cor. 6:17; John 10:28; Eph. 5:23, 30. [3] 1 Pet. 5:10; 1 Cor. 1:9.

### Question 67: What is effectual calling?

**Answer:** Effectual calling is the work of God's almighty power and grace,[1] whereby (out of his free and special love to his elect, and from nothing in them moving him thereunto)[2] he doth, in his accepted time, invite and draw them to Jesus Christ, by his word and Spirit;[3] savingly enlightening their minds,[4] renewing and powerfully determining their wills,[5] so as they (although in themselves dead in sin) are hereby made willing and able freely to answer his call, and to accept and embrace the grace offered and conveyed therein.[6]

[1] John 5:25; Eph. 1:18-20; 2 Tim. 1:8-9. [2] Titus 3:4-5; Eph. 2:4-5, 7-9. [3] 2 Cor. 5:20 compared with 2 Cor. 6:1-2; John 6:44; 2 Thess. 2:13-14. [4] Acts 26:18; 1 Cor. 2:10, 12. [5] Ezek. 11:19; Ezek. 36:26-27; John 6:45. [6] Eph. 2:5; Phil. 2:13; Deut. 30:6.

### Question 68: Are the elect only effectually called?

**Answer:** All the elect, and they only, are effectually called;[1] although others may be, and often are, outwardly called by the ministry of the word,[2] and have some common operations of the Spirit;[3] who, for their wilful neglect and contempt of the grace offered to them, being justly left in their unbelief, do never truly come to Jesus Christ.[4]

[1] Acts 13:48. [2] Matt. 22:14. [3] Matt. 7:22; Matt. 13:20-21; Heb. 6:4-6. [4] John 12:38-40; Acts 28:25-27; John 6:64-65; Psa. 81:11-12.

### Question 69: What is the communion in grace which the members of the invisible church have with Christ?

**Answer:** The communion in grace which the members of the invisible church have with Christ, is their partaking of the virtue of his mediation, in their justification,[1] adoption,[2] sanctification, and whatever else, in this life, manifests their union with him.[3]

[1] Rom. 8:30. [2] Eph. 1:5. [3] 1 Cor. 1:30.

### Question 70: What is justification?

**Answer:** Justification is an act of God's free grace unto sinners,[1] in which he pardoneth all their sins, accepteth and accounteth their persons righteous in his sight;[2] not for any thing wrought in them, or done by them,[3] but only for the perfect obedience and full satisfaction of Christ, by God imputed to them,[4] and received by faith alone.[5]

[1] Rom. 3:22, 24-25; Rom. 4:5. [2] 2 Cor. 5:19, 21; Rom. 3:22, 24-25, 27-28. [3] Titus 3:5, 7; Eph. 1:7. [4] Rom. 5:17-19; Rom. 4:6-8. [5] Acts 10:43; Gal. 2:16; Phil. 3:9.

### Question 71: How is justification an act of God's free grace?

**Answer:** Although Christ, by his obedience and death, did make a proper, real, and full satisfaction to God's justice in the behalf of them that are justified;[1] yet inasmuch as God accepteth the satisfaction from a surety, which he might have demanded of them, and did provide this surety, his own only Son,[2] imputing his righteousness to them,[3] and requiring nothing of them for their justification but faith,[4] which also is his gift,[5] their justification is to them of free grace.[6]

[1] Rom. 5:8-10, 19. [2] 1 Tim. 2:5-6; Heb. 10:10; Matt. 20:28; Dan. 9:24, 26; Isa. 53:4-6, 10-12; Heb. 7:22; Rom. 8:32; 1 Pet. 1:18-19. [3] 2 Cor. 5:21. [4] Rom. 3:24-25. [5] Eph. 2:8. [6] Eph. 1:7.

### Question 72: What is justifying faith?

**Answer:** Justifying faith is a saving grace,[1] wrought in the heart of a sinner by the Spirit[2] and word of God,[3] whereby he, being convinced of his sin and misery, and of the disability in himself and all other creatures to recover him out of his lost condition,[4] not only assenteth to the truth of the promise of the gospel,[5] but receiveth and resteth upon Christ and his righteousness, therein held forth, for pardon of sin,[6] and for the accepting and accounting of his person righteous in the sight of God for salvation.[7]

[1] Heb. 10:39. [2] 2 Cor. 4:13; Eph. 1:17-19. [3] Rom. 10:14, 17. [4] Acts 2:37; Acts 16:30; John 16:8-9; Rom. 5:6; Eph. 2:1; Acts 4:12. [5] Eph. 1:13. [6] John 1:12; Acts 16:31; Acts 10:43. [7] Phil. 3:9; Acts 15:11.

### Question 73: How doth faith justify a sinner in the sight of God?

**Answer:** Faith justifies a sinner in the sight of God, not because of those other graces which do always accompany it, or of good works that are the fruits of it,[1] nor as if the grace of faith, or any act thereof, were imputed to him for his justification;[2] but only as it is an instrument by which he receiveth and applieth Christ and his righteousness.[3]

[1] Gal. 3:11; Rom. 3:28. [2] Rom. 4:5 compared with Rom. 10:10. [3] John 1:12; Phil. 3:9; Gal. 2:16.

### Question 74: What is adoption?

**Answer:** Adoption is an act of the free grace of God,[1] in and for his only Son Jesus Christ,[2] whereby all those that are justified are received into the number of his children,[3] have his name put upon them,[4] the Spirit of his Son given to them,[5] are under his fatherly care and dispensations,[6] admitted to all the liberties and privileges of the sons of God, made heirs of all the promises, and fellow-heirs with Christ in glory.[7]

[1] 1 John 3:1. [2] Eph. 1:5; Gal. 4:4-5. [3] John 1:12. [4] 2 Cor. 6:18; Rev. 3:12. [5] Gal. 4:6. [6] Psa. 103:13; Prov. 14:26; Matt. 6:32. [7] Heb. 6:12; Rom. 8:17.

### Question 75: What is sanctification?

**Answer:** Sanctification is a work of God's grace, whereby they whom God hath, before the foundation of the world, chosen to be holy, are in time, through the powerful operation of his Spirit [1] applying the death and resurrection of Christ unto them,[2] renewed in their whole man after the image of God;[3] having the seeds of repentance unto life, and all other saving graces, put into their hearts,[4] and those graces so stirred up, increased, and strengthened,[5] as that they more and more die unto sin, and rise unto newness of life.[6]

[1] Eph. 1:4; 1 Cor. 6:11; 2 Thess. 2:13. [2] Rom. 6:4-6. [3] Eph. 4:23-24. [4] Acts 11:18; 1 John 3:9. [5] Jude 20; Heb. 6:11-12; Eph. 3:16-19; Col. 1:10-11. [6] Rom. 6:4, 6, 14; Gal. 5:24.

### Question 76: What is repentance unto life?

**Answer:** Repentance unto life is a saving grace,[1] wrought in the heart of a sinner by the Spirit [2] and word of God,[3] whereby, out of the sight and sense, not only of the danger,[4] but also of the filthiness and odiousness of his sins,[5] and upon the apprehension of God's mercy in Christ to such as are penitent,[6] he so grieves for [7] and hates his sins,[8] as that he turns from them all to God,[9] purposing and endeavouring constantly to walk with him in all the ways of new obedience.[10]

[1] 2 Tim. 2:25. [2] Zech. 12:10. [3] Acts 11:18, 20-21. [4] Ezek. 18:28, 30, 32; Luke

15:17-18; Hos. 2:6-7. [5] Ezek. 36:31; Isa. 30:22. [6] Joel 2:12-13. [7] Jer. 31:18-19. [8] 2 Cor. 7:11. [9] Acts 26:18; Ezek. 14:6; 1 Kings 8:47-48. [10] Psa. 119:6, 59, 128; Luke 1:6; 2 Kings 23:25.

## Question 77: Wherein do justification and sanctification differ?

**Answer:** Although sanctification be inseparably joined with justification,[1] yet they differ, in that God in justification imputeth the righteousness of Christ;[2] in sanctification his Spirit infuseth grace, and enableth to the exercise thereof;[3] in the former, sin is pardoned;[4] in the other, it is subdued:[5] the one doth equally free all believers from the revenging wrath of God, and that perfectly in this life, that they never fall into condemnation;[6] the other is neither equal in all,[7] nor in this life perfect in any,[8] but growing up to perfection.[9]

[1] 1 Cor. 6:11; 1 Cor. 1:30. [2] Rom. 4:6, 8. [3] Ezek. 36:27. [4] Rom. 3:24-25. [5] Rom. 6:6, 14. [6] Rom. 8:33-34. [7] 1 John 2:12-14; Heb. 5:12-14. [8] 1 John 1:8, 10. [9] 2 Cor. 7:1; Phil. 3:12-14.

## Question 78: Whence ariseth the imperfection of sanctification in believers?

**Answer:** The imperfection of sanctification in believers ariseth from the remnants of sin abiding in every part of them, and the perpetual lustings of the flesh against the spirit; whereby they are often foiled with temptations, and fall into many sins,[1] are hindered in all their spiritual services,[2] and their best works are imperfect and defiled in the sight of God.[3]

[1] Rom. 7:18, 23; Mark 14:66-72; Gal. 2:11-12. [2] Heb. 12:1. [3] Isa. 64:6; Exod. 28:38.

## Question 79: May not true believers, by reason of their imperfections, and the many temptations and sins they are overtaken with, fall away from the state of grace?

**Answer:** True believers, by reason of the unchangeable love of God,[1] and his decree and covenant to give them perseverance,[2] their inseparable union with Christ,[3] his continual intercession for them,[4] and the Spirit and seed of God abiding in them,[5] can neither totally nor finally fall away from the state of grace,[6] but are kept by the power of God through faith unto salvation.[7]

[1] Jer. 31:3. [2] 2 Tim. 2:19; Heb. 13:20-21; 2 Sam. 23:5. [3] 1 Cor. 1:8-9. [4] Heb. 7:25; Luke 22:32. [5] 1 John 3:9; 1 John 2:27. [6] Jer. 32:40; John 10:28. [7] 1 Pet. 1:5.

**Question 80: Can true believers be infallibly assured that they are in the estate of grace, and that they shall persevere therein unto salvation?**

**Answer:** Such as truly believe in Christ, and endeavour to walk in all good conscience before him,[1] may, without extraordinary revelation, by faith grounded upon the truth of God's promises, and by the Spirit enabling them to discern in themselves those graces to which the promises of life are made,[2] and bearing witness with their spirits that they are the children of God,[3] be infallibly assured that they are in the estate of grace, and shall persevere therein unto salvation.[4]

[1] 1 John 2:3. [2] 1 Cor. 2:12; 1 John 3:14, 18-19, 21, 24; 1 John 4:13, 16; Heb. 6:11-12. [3] Rom. 8:16. [4] 1 John 5:13.


**Question 81: Are all true believers at all times assured of their present being in the estate of grace, and that they shall be saved?**

**Answer:** Assurance of grace and salvation not being of the essence of faith,[1] true believers may wait long before they obtain it;[2] and, after the enjoyment thereof, may have it weakened and intermitted, through manifold distempers, sins, temptations, and desertions;[3] yet they are never left without such a presence and support of the Spirit of God as keeps them from sinking into utter despair.[4]

[1] Eph. 1:13. [2] Isa. 50:10; Psa. 88. [3] Psa. 77:1-12; Song of Sol. 5:2-3, 6; Psa. 51:8, 12; Psa. 31:22; Psa. 22:1. [4] 1 John 3:9; Job 13:15; Psa. 73:15, 23; Isa. 54:7-10.


**Question 82: What is the communion in glory which the members of the invisible church have with Christ?**

**Answer:** The communion in glory which the members of the invisible church have with Christ, is in this life,[1] immediately after death,[2] and at last perfected at the resurrection and day of judgment.[3]

[1] 2 Cor. 3:18. [2] Luke 23:43. [3] 1 Thess. 4:17.


**Question 83: What is the communion in glory with Christ which the members of the invisible church enjoy in this life?**

**Answer:** The members of the invisible church have communicated to them in this life the firstfruits of glory with Christ, as they are members of him their head, and so in him are interested in that glory which he is fully possessed of;[1] and, as an earnest thereof, enjoy the sense of God's love,[2] peace of conscience, joy in the Holy Ghost, and hope of glory;[3] as, on the contrary, sense of God's revenging wrath, horror of conscience, and a fearful expectation of judgment, are to the wicked the beginning of their torments which they shall endure after death.[4]

[1] Eph. 2:5-6. [2] Rom. 5:5; 2 Cor. 1:22. [3] Rom. 5:1-2; Rom. 14:17. [4] Gen. 4:13; Matt. 27:4; Heb. 10:27; Rom. 2:9; Mark 9:44.

### Question 84: Shall all men die?

**Answer:** Death being threatened as the wages of sin,[1] it is appointed unto all men once to die;[2] for that all have sinned.[3]

[1] Rom. 6:23. [2] Heb. 9:27. [3] Rom. 5:12.

### Question 85: Death, being the wages of sin, why are not the righteous delivered from death, seeing all their sins are forgiven in Christ?

**Answer:** The righteous shall be delivered from death itself at the last day, and even in death are delivered from the sting and curse of it;[1] so that, although they die, yet it is out of God's love,[2] to free them perfectly from sin and misery,[3] and to make them capable of further communion with Christ in glory, which they then enter upon.[4]

[1] 1 Cor. 15:26, 55-57; Heb. 2:15. [2] Isa. 57:1-2; 2 Kings 22:20. [3] Rev. 14:13; Eph. 5:27. [4] Luke 23:43; Phil. 1:23.

### Question 86: What is the communion in glory with Christ, which the members of the invisible church enjoy immediately after death?

**Answer:** The communion in glory with Christ, which the members of the invisible church enjoy immediately after death, is, in that their souls are then made perfect in holiness,[1] and received into the highest heavens,[2] where they behold the face of God in light and glory,[3] waiting for the full redemption of their bodies,[4] which even in death continue united to Christ,[5] and rest in their graves as in their beds,[6] till at the last day they be again united to their souls.[7] Whereas the souls of the wicked are at their death cast into hell, where they remain in torments and utter darkness, and their bodies kept in their graves, as in their prisons, till the resurrection and judgment of the great day.[8]

[1] Heb. 12:23. [2] 2 Cor. 5:1, 6, 8; Phil. 1:23 compared with Acts 3:21 and with Eph. 4:10. [3] 1 John 3:2; 1 Cor. 13:12. [4] Rom. 8:23; Psa. 16:9. [5] 1 Thess. 4:14. [6] Isa. 57:2. [7] Job 19:26-27. [8] Luke 16:23-24; Acts 1:25; Jude 6-7.

**Question 87: What are we to believe concerning the resurrection?**

**Answer:** We are to believe, that at the last day there shall be a general resurrection of the dead, both of the just and unjust:[1] when they that are then found alive shall in a moment be changed; and the selfsame bodies of the dead which were laid in the grave, being then again united to their souls forever, shall be raised up by the power of Christ.[2] The bodies of the just, by the Spirit of Christ, and by virtue of his resurrection as their head, shall be raised in power, spiritual, incorruptible, and made like to his glorious body;[3] and the bodies of the wicked shall be raised up in dishonour by him, as an offended judge.[4]

[1] Acts 24:15. [2] 1 Cor. 15:51-53; 1 Thess. 4:15-17; John 5:28-29. [3] 1 Cor. 15:21-23, 42-44; Phil. 3:21. [4] John 5:27-29; Matt. 25:33.

**Question 88: What shall immediately follow after the resurrection?**

**Answer:** Immediately after the resurrection shall follow the general and final judgment of angels and men;[1] the day and hour whereof no man knoweth, that all may watch and pray, and be ever ready for the coming of the Lord.[2]

[1] 2 Pet. 2:4; Jude 6-7, 14-15; Matt. 25:46. [2] Matt. 24:36, 42, 44; Luke 21:35-36.

**Question 89: What shall be done to the wicked at the day of judgment?**

**Answer:** At the day of judgment, the wicked shall be set on Christ's left hand,[1] and, upon clear evidence, and full conviction of their own consciences,[2] shall have the fearful but just sentence of condemnation pronounced against them;[3] and thereupon shall be cast out from the favourable presence of God, and the glorious fellowship with Christ, his saints, and all his holy angels, into hell, to be punished with unspeakable torments, both of body and soul, with the devil and his angels forever.[4]

[1] Matt. 25:33. [2] Rom. 2:15-16. [3] Matt. 25:41-43. [4] Luke 16:26; 2 Thess. 1:8-9.

**Question 90: What shall be done to the righteous at the day of judgment?**

**Answer:** At the day of judgment, the righteous, being caught up to Christ in the clouds,[1] shall be set on his right hand, and there openly acknowledged and acquitted,[2] shall join with him in the judging of reprobate angels and men,[3] and shall be received into heaven,[4] where they shall be fully and forever freed from all sin and misery;[5] filled with inconceivable joys,[6] made perfectly holy and happy both in body and soul, in the company of innumerable saints and holy angels,[7] but especially in the immediate vision and fruition of God the Father, of our Lord Jesus Christ, and of the Holy Spirit, to all eternity.[8] And this is the perfect and full communion, which the members of the invisible church shall enjoy with Christ in glory, at the resurrection and day of judgment.

[1] 1 Thess. 4:17. [2] Matt. 25:33; Matt. 10:32. [3] 1 Cor. 6:2-3. [4] Matt. 25:34, 46. [5] Eph. 5:27; Rev. 14:13. [6] Psa. 16:11. [7] Heb. 12:22-23. [8] 1 John 3:2; 1 Cor. 13:12; 1 Thess. 4:17-18.

## HAVING SEEN WHAT THE SCRIPTURES PRINCIPALLY TEACH US TO BELIEVE CONCERNING GOD, IT FOLLOWS TO CONSIDER WHAT THEY REQUIRE AS THE DUTY OF MAN

### Question 91: What is the duty which God requireth of man?

**Answer:** The duty which God requireth of man, is obedience to his revealed will.[1]

[1] Rom. 12:1-2; Mic. 6:8; 1 Sam. 15:22.

### Question 92: What did God at first reveal unto man as the rule of his obedience?

**Answer:** The rule of obedience revealed to Adam in the estate of innocence, and to all mankind in him, besides a special command not to eat of the fruit of the tree of knowledge of good and evil, was the moral law.[1]

[1] Gen. 1:26-27; Rom. 2:14-15; Rom. 10:5; Gen. 2:17.

### Question 93: What is the moral law?

**Answer:** The moral law is the declaration of the will of God to mankind, directing and binding every one to personal, perfect, and perpetual conformity and obedience thereunto, in the frame and disposition of the whole man, soul and body,[1] and in performance of all those duties of holiness and righteousness which he oweth to God and man:[2] promising life upon the fulfilling, and threatening death upon the breach of it.[3]

[1] Deut. 5:1-3, 31, 33; Luke 10:26-27; Gal. 3:10; 1 Thess. 5:23. [2] Luke 1:75; Acts 24:16. [3] Rom. 10:5; Gal. 3:10. 12.

**Question 94: Is there any use of the moral law to man since the fall?**

**Answer:** Although no man, since the fall, can attain to righteousness and life by the moral law;[1] yet there is great use thereof, as well common to all men, as peculiar either to the unregenerate, or the regenerate.[2]

[1] Rom. 8:3; Gal. 2:16. [2] 1 Tim. 1:8.


**Question 95: Of what use is the moral law to all men?**

**Answer:** The moral law is of use to all men, to inform them of the holy nature and the will of God,[1] and of their duty, binding them to walk accordingly;[2] to convince them of their disability to keep it, and of the sinful pollution of their nature, hearts, and lives:[3] to humble them in the sense of their sin and misery,[4] and thereby help them to a clearer sight of the need they have of Christ,[5] and of the perfection of his obedience.[6]

[1] Lev. 11:44-45; Lev. 20:7-8; Rom. 7:12. [2] Mic. 6:8; James 2:10-11. [3] Psa. 19:11-12; Rom. 3:20; Rom. 7:7. [4] Rom. 3:9, 23. [5] Gal. 3:21-22. [6] Rom. 10:4.


**Question 96: What particular use is there of the moral law to unregenerate men?**

**Answer:** The moral law is of use to unregenerate men, to awaken their consciences to flee from wrath to come,[1] and to drive them to Christ;[2] or, upon their continuance in the estate and way of sin, to leave them inexcusable,[3] and under the curse thereof.[4]

[1] 1 Tim. 1:9-10. [2] Gal. 3:24. [3] Rom. 1:20 compared with Rom. 2:15; [4] Gal. 3:10.


**Question 97: What special use is there of the moral law to the regenerate?**

**Answer:** Although they that are regenerate, and believe in Christ, be delivered from the moral law as a covenant of works,[1] so as thereby they are neither justified[2] nor condemned;[3] yet, besides the general uses thereof common to them with all men, it is of special use, to show them how much they are bound to Christ for his fulfilling it, and enduring the curse thereof in their stead, and for their good;[4] and thereby to provoke them to more thankfulness,[5] and to express the same in their greater care to conform themselves thereunto as the rule of their obedience.[6]

[1] Rom. 6:14; Rom. 7:4, 6; Gal. 4:4-5. [2] Rom. 3:20; [3] Gal. 5:23; Rom. 8:1. [4] Rom. 7:24-25; Gal. 3:13-14; Rom. 8:3-4. [5] Luke 1:68-69, 74-75; Col. 1:12-14. [6] Rom. 7:22; Rom. 12:2; Titus 2:11-14.

**Question 98: Where is the moral law summarily comprehended?**

**Answer:** The moral law is summarily comprehended in the ten commandments, which were delivered by the voice of God upon Mount Sinai, and written by him in two tables of stone;[1] and are recorded in the twentieth chapter of Exodus. The four first commandments containing our duty to God, and the other six our duty to man.[2]

[1] Deut. 10:4; Exod. 34:1-4. [2] Matt. 22:37-40.

**Question 99: What rules are to be observed for the right understanding of the ten commandments?**

**Answer:** For the right understanding of the ten commandments, these rules are to be observed:

**1.** That the law is perfect, and bindeth everyone to full conformity in the whole man unto the righteousness thereof, and unto entire obedience forever; so as to require the utmost perfection of every duty, and to forbid the least degree of every sin.[1]

[1] Psa. 19:7; James 2:10; Matt. 5:21-22.

**2.** That it is spiritual, and so reacheth the understanding, will, affections, and all other powers of the soul; as well as words, works, and gestures.[1]

[1] Rom. 7:14; Deut. 6:5 compared with Matt. 22:37-39; Matt. 5:21-22, 27-28, 33-34, 38-39, 43-44.

**3.** That one and the same thing, in divers respects, is required or forbidden in several commandments.[1]

[1] Col. 3:5; Amos 8:5; Prov. 1:19; 1 Tim. 6:10.

**4.** That as, where a duty is commanded, the contrary sin is forbidden;[1] and, where a sin is forbidden, the contrary duty is commanded:[2] so, where a promise is annexed, the contrary threatening is included;[3] and, where a threatening is annexed, the contrary promise is included.[4]

[1] Isa. 58:13; Deut. 6:13 compared with Matt. 4:9-10; Matt. 15:4-6. [2] Matt. 5:21-25; Eph. 4:28. [3] Exod. 20:12 compared with Prov. 30:17. [4] Jer. 18:7-8; Exod. 20:7 compared with Psa. 15:1, 4-5 and with Psa. 24:4-5.

**5.** That what God forbids, is at no time to be done;[1] what he commands, is always our duty;[2] and yet every particular duty is not to be done at all times.[3]

[1] Job 13:7-8; Rom. 3:8; Job 36:21; Heb. 11:25. [2] Deut. 4:8-9. [3] Matt. 12:7.

**6.** That under one sin or duty, all of the same kind are forbidden or commanded; together with all the causes, means, occasions, and appearances thereof, and provocations thereunto.[1]

[1] Matt. 5:21-22, 27-28; Matt. 15:4-6; Heb. 10:24-25; 1 Thess. 5:22; Jude 23; Gal. 5:26; Col. 3:21.

**7.** That what is forbidden or commanded to ourselves, we are bound, according to our places to endeavour that it may be avoided or performed by others, according to the duty of their places.[1]

[1] Exod. 20:10; Lev. 19:17; Gen. 18:19; Josh. 24:15; Deut. 6:6-7.

**8.** That in what is commanded to others, we are bound, according to our places and callings, to be helpful to them;[1] and to take heed of partaking with others in what is forbidden them.[2]

[1] 2 Cor. 1:24. [2] 1 Tim. 5:22; Eph. 5:11.

### Question 100: What special things are we to consider in the ten commandments?

**Answer:** We are to consider, in the ten commandments, the preface, the substance of the commandments themselves, and several reasons annexed to some of them, the more to enforce them.

### Question 101: What is the preface to the ten commandments?

**Answer:** The preface to the ten commandments is contained in these words, *I am the Lord thy God, which have brought thee out of the land of Egypt, out of the house of bondage.*[1] Wherein God manifesteth his sovereignty, as being JEHOVAH, the eternal, immutable, and almighty God;[2] having his being in and of himself,[3] and giving being to all his words[4] and works:[5] and that he is a God in covenant, as with Israel of old, so with all his people;[6] who, as he brought them out of their bondage in Egypt, so he delivereth us from our spiritual thraldom;[7] and that therefore we are bound to take him for our God alone, and to keep all his commandments.[8]

[1] Exod. 20:2. [2] Isa. 44:6. [3] Exod. 3:14. [4] Exod. 6:3. [5] Acts 17:24, 28. [6] Gen. 17:7 compared with Rom. 3:29. [7] Luke 1:74-75 [8] 1 Pet. 1:15-18; Lev. 18:30; Lev. 19:37.

**Question 102: What is the sum of the four commandments which contain our duty to God?**

**Answer:** The sum of the four commandments containing our duty to God is, to love the Lord our God with all our heart, and with all our soul, and with all our strength, and with all our mind.[1]

[1] Luke 10:27.


**Question 103: Which is the first commandment?**

**Answer:** The first commandment is, *Thou shalt have no other gods before me.*[1]

[1] Exod. 20:3.


**Question 104: What are the duties required in the first commandment?**

**Answer:** The duties required in the first commandment are, the knowing and acknowledging of God to be the only true God, and our God;[1] and to worship and glorify him accordingly,[2] by thinking,[3] meditating,[4] remembering,[5] highly esteeming,[6] honouring,[7] adoring,[8] choosing,[9] loving,[10] desiring,[11] fearing of him;[12] believing him;[13] trusting,[14] hoping,[15] delighting,[16] rejoicing in him;[17] being zealous for him;[18] calling upon him, giving all praise and thanks,[19] and yielding all obedience and submission to him with the whole man;[20] being careful in all things to please him,[21] and sorrowful when in any thing he is offended;[22] and walking humbly with him.[23]

[1] 1 Chron. 28:9; Deut. 26:17; Isa. 43:10; Jer. 14:22. [2] Psa. 95:6-7; Matt. 4:10; Psa. 29:2. [3] Mal. 3:16. [4] Psa. 63:6. [5] Eccles. 12:1. [6] Psa. 71:19. [7] Mal. 1:6. [8] Isa. 45:23. [9] Josh. 24:15, 22. [10] Deut. 6:5. [11] Psa. 73:25. [12] Isa. 8:13. [13] Exod. 14:31. [14] Isa. 26:4. [15] Psa. 130:7. [16] Psa. 37:4. [17] Psa. 32:11. [18] Rom. 12:11 compared with Num. 25:11. [19] Phil. 4:6. [20] Jer. 7:23; James 4:7. [21] 1 John 3:22. [22] Jer. 31:18; Psa. 119:136. [23] Mic. 6:8.


**Question 105: What are the sins forbidden in the first commandment?**

**Answer:** The sins forbidden in the first commandment, are, atheism, in denying or not having a God;[1] idolatry, in having or worshipping more gods than one, or any with or instead of the true God;[2] the not having and avouching him for God, and our God;[3] the omission or neglect of anything due to him, required in this commandment;[4] ignorance,[5] forgetfulness,[6] misapprehensions,[7] false opinions,[8] unworthy and wicked thoughts of him;[9] bold and curious searching into his secrets;[10] all profaneness,[11] hatred of God;[12] self-love,[13] self-seeking,[14] and all other inordinate and immoderate setting of our mind, will, or affections upon other things, and taking them off from him in whole or in part;[15] vain credulity,[16] unbelief,[17] heresy,[18] misbelief,[19] distrust,[20] despair,[21] incorrigibleness,[22] and insensibleness under judgments,[23] hardness of heart,[24] pride,[25] presumption,[26] carnal security,[27] tempting of God;[28] using unlawful means,[29] and trusting in lawful means;[30] carnal delights and joys;[31] corrupt, blind, and indiscreet zeal;[32] lukewarmness,[33] and deadness in the things of God;[34] estranging ourselves, and apostatizing from God;[35] praying, or giving any religious worship, to saints, angels, or any other creatures;[36] all compacts and consulting with the devil,[37] and hearkening to his suggestions;[38] making men the lords of our faith and conscience;[39] slighting and despising God and his commands;[40] resisting and grieving of his Spirit,[41] discontent and impatience at his dispensations, charging him foolishly for the evils he inflicts on us;[42] and ascribing the praise of any good we either are, have, or can do, to fortune,[43] idols,[44] ourselves,[45] or any other creature.[46]

[1] Psa. 14:1; Eph. 2:12. [2] Jer. 2:27-28 compared with 1 Thess. 1:9. [3] Psa. 81:11. [4] Isa. 43:22-24. [5] Jer. 4:22; Hos. 4:1, 6. [6] Jer. 2:32. [7] Acts 17:23, 29. [8] Isa. 40:18. [9] Psa. 50:21. [10] Deut. 29:29. [11] Titus 1:16; Heb. 12:16. [12] Rom. 1:30. [13] 2 Tim. 3:2. [14] Phil. 2:21. [15] 1 John 2:15-16; 1 Sam. 2:29; Col. 3:2, 5. [16] 1 John 4:1. [17] Heb. 3:12. [18] Gal. 5:20; Titus 3:10. [19] Acts 26:9. [20] Psa. 78:22. [21] Gen. 4:13. [22] Jer. 5:3. [23] Isa. 42:25. [24] Rom. 2:5. [25] Jer. 13:15. [26] Psa. 19:13. [27] Zeph. 1:12. [28] Matt. 4:7. [9] Rom. 3:8. [30] Jer. 17:5. [31] 2 Tim. 3:4. [32] Gal. 4:17; John 16:2; Rom. 10:2; Luke 9:54-55. [33] Rev. 3:16. [34] Rev. 3:1. [35] Ezek. 14:5; Isa. 1:4-5. [36] Rom. 10:13-14; Hos. 4:12; Acts 10:25-26; Rev. 19:10; Matt. 4:10; Col. 2:18; Rom. 1:25. [37] Lev. 20:6; 1 Sam. 28:7, 11 compared with 1 Chron. 10:13-14. [38] Acts 5:3. [9] 2 Cor. 1:24; Matt. 23:9. [40] Deut. 32:15; 2 Sam. 12:9; Prov. 13:13. [41] Acts 7:51; Eph. 4:30. [42] Psa. 73:2-3, 13-15, 22; Job 1:22. [43] 1 Sam. 6:7-9. [44] Dan. 5:23. [45] Deut. 8:17; Dan. 4:30. [46] Hab. 1:16.

### Question 106: What are we specially taught by these words [*before me*] in the first commandment?

**Answer:** These words [*before me*] or before my face, in the first commandment, teach us, that God, who seeth all things, taketh special notice of, and is much displeased with, the sin of having any other God: that so it may be an argument to dissuade from it, and to aggravate it as a most impudent provocation:[1] as also to persuade us to do as in his sight, whatever we do in his service.[2]

[1] Ezek. 8:5-18; Psa. 44:20-21. [2] 1 Chron. 28:9.

**Question 107: Which is the second commandment?**

**Answer:** The second commandment is, *Thou shalt not make unto thee any graven image, or any likeness of any thing that is in heaven above, or that is in the earth beneath, or that is in the water under the earth. Thou shalt not bow down thyself to them, nor serve them: for I the Lord thy God am a jealous God, visiting the iniquity of the fathers upon the children unto the third and fourth generation of them that hate me; and showing mercy unto thousands of them that love me, and keep my commandments.*[1]

[1] Exod. 20:4-6.

**Question 108: What are the duties required in the second commandment?**

**Answer:** The duties required in the second commandment are, the receiving, observing, and keeping pure and entire, all such religious worship and ordinances as God hath instituted in his word;[1] particularly prayer and thanksgiving in the name of Christ;[2] the reading, preaching, and hearing of the word;[3] the administration and receiving of the sacraments;[4] church government and discipline;[5] the ministry and maintenance thereof;[6] religious fasting;[7] swearing by the name of God;[8] and vowing unto him;[9] as also the disapproving, detesting, opposing all false worship;[10] and, according to each one's place and calling, removing it, and all monuments of idolatry.[11]

[1] Deut. 32:46-47; Matt. 28:20; Acts 2:42; 1 Tim. 6:13-14. [2] Phil. 4:6; Eph. 5:20. [3] Deut. 17:18-19; Acts 15:21; 2 Tim. 4:2; James 1:21-22; Acts 10:33. [4] Matt. 28:19; 1 Cor. 11:23-30. [5] Matt. 18:15-17; Matt. 16:19; 1 Cor. 5; 1 Cor. 12:28. [6] Eph. 4:11-12; 1 Tim. 5:17-18; 1 Cor. 9:7-15. [7] Joel 2:12-13; 1 Cor. 7:5. [8] Deut. 6:13. [9] Isa. 19:21; Psa. 76:11. [10] Acts 17:16-17; Psa. 16:4. [11] Deut. 7:5; Isa. 30:22.

**Question 109: What are the sins forbidden in the second commandment?**

**Answer:** The sins forbidden in the second commandment are, all devising,[1] counselling,[2] commanding,[3] using,[4] and anywise approving, any religious worship not instituted by God himself;[5] tolerating a false religion;[6] the making any representation of God, of all or of any of the three persons, either inwardly in our mind, or outwardly in any kind of image or likeness of any creature whatsoever;[7] all worshipping of it,[8] or God in it or by it;[9] the making of any representation of feigned deities,[10] and all worship of them, or service belonging to them;[11] all superstitious devices,[12] corrupting the worship of God,[13] adding to it, or taking from it,[14] whether invented and taken up of ourselves,[15] or received by tradition from others,[16] though under the title of antiquity,[17] custom,[18] devotion,[19] good intent, or any other pretence whatsoever;[20] simony;[21] sacrilege;[22] all neglect,[23] contempt,[24] hindering,[25] and opposing the worship and ordinances which God hath appointed.[26]

[1] Num. 15:39. [2] Deut. 13:6-8. [3] Hos. 5:11; Mic. 6:16. [4] 1 Kings 11:33; 1 Kings 12:33. [5] Deut. 12:30-32. [6] Deut. 13:6-12; Zech. 13:2-3; Rev. 2:2, 14-15, 20; Rev. 17:12, 16-17. [7] Deut. 4:15-19; Acts 17:29; Rom. 1:21-23, 25. [8] Dan. 3:18; Gal. 4:8. [9] Exod. 32:5. [10] Exod. 32:8. [11] 1 Kings 18:26, 28; Isa. 65:11. [12] Acts 17:22; Col. 2:21-23. [13] Mal. 1:7-8, 14. [14] Deut. 4:2. [15] Psa. 106:39. [16] Matt. 15:9. [17] 1 Pet. 1:18. [18] Jer. 44:17. [19] Isa. 65:3-5; Gal. 1:13-14. [20] 1 Sam. 13:11-12; 1 Sam. 15:21. [21] Acts 8:18. [22] Rom. 2:22; Mal. 3:8. [23] Exod. 4:24-26. [24] Matt. 22:5; Mal. 1:7, 13. [25] Matt. 23:13. [26] Acts 13:44-45; 1 Thess. 2:15-16.

### Question 110: What are the reasons annexed to the second commandment, the more to enforce it?

**Answer:** The reasons annexed to the second commandment, the more to enforce it, contained in these words, *For I the Lord thy God am a jealous God, visiting the iniquity of the fathers upon the children unto the third and fourth generation of them that hate me; and shewing mercy unto thousands of them that love me, and keep my commandments;*[1] are, besides God's sovereignty over us, and propriety in us,[2] his fervent zeal for his own worship,[3] and his revengeful indignation against all false worship, as being a spiritual whoredom;[4] accounting the breakers of this commandment such as hate him, and threatening to punish them unto divers generations;[5] and esteeming the observers of it such as love him and keep his commandments, and promising mercy to them unto many generations.[6]

[1] Exod. 20:5-6. [2] Psa. 45:11; Rev. 15:3-4. [3] Exod. 34:13-14. [4] 1 Cor. 10:20-22; Jer. 7:18-20; Ezek. 16:26-27; Deut. 32:16-20. [5] Hos. 2:2-4. [6] Deut. 5:29.

### Question 111: Which is the third commandment?

**Answer:** The third commandment is, *Thou shalt not take the name of the Lord thy God in vain: for the Lord will not hold him guiltless that taketh his name in vain.*[1]

[1] Exod. 20:7.

### Question 112: What is required in the third commandment?

**Answer:** The third commandment requires, That the name of God, his titles, attributes,[1] ordinances,[2] the word,[3] sacraments,[4] prayer,[5] oaths,[6] vows,[7] lots,[8] his works,[9] and whatsoever else there is whereby he makes himself known, be holily and reverently used in thought,[10] meditation,[11] word,[12] and writing;[13] by an holy profession,[14] and answerable conversation,[15] to the glory of God,[16] and the good of ourselves,[17] and others.[18]

[1] Matt. 6:9; Deut. 28:58; Psa. 29:2; Psa. 68:4; Rev. 15:3-4. [2] Mal. 1:14; Eccles. 5:1. [3] Psa. 138:2. [4] 1 Cor. 11:24-25, 28-29. [5] 1 Tim. 2:8. [6] Jer. 4:2. [7] Eccles. 5:2, 4-6. [8] Acts 1:24, 26. [9] Job 36:24. [10] Mal. 3:16. [11] Psa. 8. [12] Col. 3:17; Psa. 105:2, 5. [13] Psa. 102:18. [14] 1 Pet. 3:15; Mic. 4:5. [15] Phil. 1:27. [16] 1 Cor. 10:31. [17] Jer. 32:39. [18] 1 Pet. 2:12.


### Question 113: What are the sins forbidden in the third commandment?

**Answer:** The sins forbidden in the third commandment are, the not using of God's name as is required;[1] and the abuse of it in an ignorant,[2] vain,[3] irreverent, profane,[4] superstitious[5] or wicked mentioning or otherwise using his titles, attributes,[6] ordinances,[7] or works,[8] by blasphemy,[9] perjury;[10] all sinful cursings,[11] oaths,[12] vows,[13] and lots;[14] violating of our oaths and vows, if lawful;[15] and fulfilling them, if of things unlawful;[16] murmuring and quarrelling at,[17] curious prying into,[18] and misapplying of God's decrees[19] and providences;[20] misinterpreting,[21] misapplying,[22] or any way perverting the word, or any part of it,[23] to profane jests,[24] curious or unprofitable questions, vain janglings, or the maintaining of false doctrines;[25] abusing it, the creatures, or anything contained under the name of God, to charms,[26] or sinful lusts and practices;[27] the maligning,[28] scorning,[29] reviling,[30] or any wise opposing of God's truth, grace, and ways;[31] making profession of religion in hypocrisy, or for sinister ends;[32] being ashamed of it,[33] or a shame to it, by unconformable,[34] unwise,[35] unfruitful,[36] and offensive walking,[37] or backsliding from it.[38]

[1] Mal. 2:2. [2] Acts 17:23. [3] Prov. 30:9. [4] Mal. 1:6-7, 12; Mal. 3:14. [5] 1 Sam. 4:3-5; Jer. 7:4, 9-10, 14, 31; Col. 2:20-22. [6] 2 Kings 18:30, 35; Exod. 5:2; Psa. 139:20. [7] Psa. 50:16-17. [8] Isa. 5:12. [9] 2 Kings 19:22; Lev. 24:11. [10] Zech. 5:4; Zech. 8:17. [11] 1 Sam. 17:43; 2 Sam. 16:5. [12] Jer. 5:7; Jer. 23:10. [13] Deut. 23:18; Acts 23:12, 14. [14] Esther 3:7; Esther 9:24; Psa. 22:18. [15] Psa. 24:4; Ezek. 17:16, 18-19. [16] Mark 6:26; 1 Sam. 25:22, 32-34. [17] Rom. 9:14, 19-20. [18] Deut. 29:29. [19] Rom. 3:5, 7; Rom. 6:1-2. [20] Eccles. 8:11; Eccles. 9:3; Psa. 39. [21] Matt. 5:21-48. [22] Ezek. 13:22. [23] 2 Pet. 3:16; Matt. 22:24-31. [24] Isa. 22:13; Jer. 23:34, 36, 38. [25] 1 Tim. 1:4, 6-7; 1 Tim. 6:4-5, 20; 2 Tim. 2:14; Titus 3:9. [26] Deut. 18:10-14; Acts 19:13. [27] 2 Tim. 4:3-4; Rom. 13:13-14; 1 Kings 21:9-10; Jude 4. [28] Acts 13:45; 1 John 3:12. [29] Psa. 1:1; 2 Pet. 3:3. [30] 1 Pet. 4:4. [31] Acts 13:45-46, 50; Acts 4:18; Acts 19:9; 1 Thess. 2:16; Heb. 10:29. [32] 2 Tim. 3:5; Matt. 23:14; Matt. 6:1-2, 5, 16. [33] Mark 8:38.

[34] Psa. 73:14. [35] 1 Cor. 6:5-6; Eph. 5:15-17. [36] Isa. 5:4; 2 Pet. 1:8-9. [37] Rom. 2:23-24. [38] Gal. 3:1, 3; Heb. 6:6.

### Question 114: What reasons are annexed to the third commandment?

**Answer:** The reasons annexed to the third commandment, in these words, *The Lord thy God*, and, *For the Lord will not hold him guiltless that taketh his name in vain*,[1] are, because he is the Lord and our God, therefore his name is not to be profaned, or any way abused by us;[2] especially because he will be so far from acquitting and sparing the transgressors of this commandment, as that he will not suffer them to escape his righteous judgment,[3] albeit many such escape the censures and punishments of men.[4]

[1] Exod. 20:7. [2] Lev. 19:12. [3] Ezek. 36:21-23; Deut. 28:58-59; Zech. 5:2-4. [4] 1 Sam. 2:12, 17, 22, 24 compared with 1 Sam. 3:13.

### Question 115: Which is the fourth commandment?

**Answer:** The fourth commandment is, *Remember the sabbath day, to keep it holy. Six days shalt thou labour, and do all thy work; but the seventh day is the sabbath of the Lord thy God: in it thou shalt not do any work, thou, nor thy son, nor thy daughter, thy man-servant, nor thy maid-servant, nor thy cattle, nor thy stranger that is within thy gates. For in six days the Lord made heaven and earth, the sea, and all that in them is, and rested in the seventh day: wherefore the Lord blessed the sabbath-day and hallowed it.*[1]

[1] Exod. 20:8-11.

### Question 116: What is required in the fourth commandment?

**Answer:** The fourth commandment requireth of all men the sanctifying or keeping holy to God such set times as he hath appointed in his word, expressly one whole day in seven; which was the seventh from the beginning of the world to the resurrection of Christ, and the first day of the week ever since, and so to continue to the end of the world; which is the Christian sabbath,[1] and in the New Testament called *The Lord's day*.[2]

[1] Deut. 5:12-14; Gen. 2:2-3; 1 Cor. 16:1-2; Acts 20:7; Matt. 5:17-18; Isa. 56:2, 4, 6-7. [2] Rev. 1:10.

### Question 117: How is the sabbath or the Lord's day to be sanctified?

**Answer:** The sabbath or Lord's day is to be sanctified by an holy resting all the day,[1] not only from such works as are at all times sinful, but even from such worldly employments and recreations as are on other days lawful;[2] and making it our delight to spend the whole time (except so much of it as is to be taken up in works of necessity and mercy)[3] in the public and private exercises of God's worship:[4] and, to that end, we are to prepare our hearts, and with such foresight, diligence, and moderation, to dispose and season-ably dispatch our worldly business, that we may be the more free and fit for the duties of that day.[5]

[1] Exod. 20:8, 10. [2] Exod. 16:25-28; Neh. 13:15-22; Jer. 17:21-22. [3] Matt. 12:1-13. [4] Isa. 58:13; Luke 4:16; Acts 20:7; 1 Cor. 16:1-2; Psa. 92 [title, *A Psalm or Song for the Sabbath Day*]; Isa. 66:23; Lev. 23:3. [5] Exod. 20:8; Luke 23:54, 56; Exod. 16:22, 25-26, 29; Neh. 13:19.

### Question 118: Why is the charge of keeping the sabbath more specially directed to governors of families, and other superiors?

**Answer:** The charge of keeping the sabbath is more specially directed to governors of families, and other superiors, because they are bound not only to keep it themselves, but to see that it be observed by all those that are under their charge; and because they are prone ofttimes to hinder them by employments of their own.[1]

[1] Exod. 20:10; Josh. 24:15; Neh. 13:15, 17; Jer. 17:20-22; Exod. 23:12.

### Question 119: What are the sins forbidden in the fourth commandment?

**Answer:** The sins forbidden in the fourth commandment are, all omissions of the duties required,[1] all careless, negligent, and unprofitable performing of them, and being weary of them;[2] all profaning the day by idleness, and doing that which is in itself sinful;[3] and by all needless works, words, and thoughts, about our worldly employments and recreations.[4]

[1] Ezek. 22:26. [2] Acts 20:7, 9; Ezek. 33:30-32; Amos 8:5; Mal. 1:13. [3] Ezek. 23:38. [4] Jer. 17:24, 27; Isa. 58:13.

### Question 120: What are the reasons annexed to the fourth command-ment, the more to enforce it?

**Answer:** The reasons annexed to the fourth commandment, the more to enforce it, are taken from the equity of it, God allowing us six days of seven for our own affairs, and reserving but one for himself in these words, *Six days shalt thou labour, and do all thy work:*[1] from God's challenging a special propriety in that day, *The seventh day is the sabbath of the Lord thy God:*[2]

from the example of God, who *in six days made heaven and earth, the sea, and all that in them is, and rested the seventh day:* and from that blessing which God put upon that day, not only in sanctifying it to be a day for his service, but in ordaining it to be a means of blessing to us in our sanctifying it; *Wherefore the Lord blessed the sabbath day, and hallowed it.*[3]

[1] Exod. 20:9. [2] Exod. 20:10. [3] Exod. 20:11.


### Question 121: Why is the word *Remember* set in the beginning of the fourth commandment?

**Answer:** The word *Remember* is set in the beginning of the fourth commandment,[1] partly, because of the great benefit of remembering it, we being thereby helped in our preparation to keep it,[2] and, in keeping it, better to keep all the rest of the commandments,[3] and to continue a thankful remembrance of the two great benefits of creation and redemption, which contain a short abridgment of religion;[4] and partly, because we are very ready to forget it,[5] for that there is less light of nature for it,[6] and yet it restraineth our natural liberty in things at other times lawful;[7] that it cometh but once in seven days, and many worldly businesses come between, and too often take off our minds from thinking of it, either to prepare for it, or to sanctify it;[8] and that Satan with his instruments much labour to blot out the glory, and even the memory of it, to bring in all irreligion and impiety.[9]

[1] Exod. 20:8. [2] Exod. 16:23; Luke 23:54, 56 compared with Mark 15:42; Neh. 13:19. [3] Psa. 92 [title, *A Psalm or Song for the Sabbath Day*] compared with Psa. 92:13-14; Ezek. 20:12, 19-20. [4] Gen. 2:2-3; Psa. 118:22, 24 compared with Acts 4:10-11; Rev. 1:10. [5] Ezek. 22:26. [6] Neh. 9:14. [7] Exod. 34:21. [8] Deut. 5:14-15; Amos 8:5. [9] Lam. 1:7; Jer. 17:21-23; Neh. 13:15-23.


### Question 122: What is the sum of the six commandments which contain our duty to man?

**Answer:** The sum of the six commandments which contain our duty to man, is, to love our neighbour as ourselves,[1] and to do to others what we would have them to do to us.[2]

[1] Matt. 22:39. [2] Matt. 7:12.


### Question 123: Which is the fifth commandment?

**Answer:** The fifth commandment is, *Honour thy father and thy mother: that thy days may be long upon the land which the Lord thy God giveth thee.*[1]

[1] Exod. 20:12.

**Question 124: Who are meant by *father* and *mother* in the fifth commandment?**

**Answer:** By *father* and *mother,* in the fifth commandment, are meant, not only natural parents,[1] but all superiors in age[2] and gifts;[3] and especially such as, by God's ordinance, are over us in place of authority, whether in family,[4] church,[5] or commonwealth.[6]

[1] Prov. 23:22, 25; Eph. 6:1-2. [2] 1 Tim. 5:1-2. [3] Gen. 4:20-22; Gen. 45:8. [4] 2 Kings 5:13. [5] 2 Kings 2:12; 2 Kings 13:14; Gal. 4:19. [6] Isa. 49:23.

**Question 125: Why are superiors styled *Father* and *Mother*?**

**Answer:** Superiors are styled *Father* and *Mother,* both to teach them in all duties toward their inferiors, like natural parents, to express love and tenderness to them, according to their several relations;[1] and to work inferiors to a greater willingness and cheerfulness in performing their duties to their superiors, as to their parents.[2]

[1] Eph. 6:4; 2 Cor. 12:14; 1 Thess. 2:7-8, 11; Num. 11:11-12. [2] 1 Cor. 4:14-16; 2 Kings 5:13.

**Question 126: What is the general scope of the fifth commandment?**

**Answer:** The general scope of the fifth commandment is, the performance of those duties which we mutually owe in our several relations, as inferiors, superiors, or equals.[1]

[1] Eph. 5:21; 1 Pet. 2:17; Rom. 12:10.

**Question 127: What is the honour that inferiors owe to their superiors?**

**Answer:** The honour which inferiors owe to their superiors is, all due reverence in heart,[1] word,[2] and behaviour;[3] prayer and thanksgiving for them;[4] imitation of their virtues and graces;[5] willing obedience to their lawful commands and counsels;[6] due submission to their corrections;[7] fidelity to,[8] defence,[9] and maintenance of their persons and authority, according to their several ranks, and the nature of their places;[10] bearing with their infirmities, and covering them in love,[11] that so they may be an honour to them and to their government.[12]

[1] Mal. 1:6; Lev. 19:3. [2] Prov. 31:28; 1 Pet. 3:6. [3] Lev. 19:32; 1 Kings 2:19. [4] 1 Tim. 2:1-2. [5] Heb. 13:7; Phil. 3:17. [6] Eph. 6:1-2, 5-7; 1 Pet. 2:13-14; Rom. 13:1-5; Heb. 13:17; Prov. 4:3-4; Prov. 23:22; Exod. 18:19, 24. [7] Heb. 12:9; 1 Pet. 2:18-20. [8] Titus 2:9-10. [9] 1 Sam. 26:15-16; 2 Sam. 18:3; Esther 6:2. [10] Matt. 22:21; Rom.

13:6-7; 1 Tim. 5:17-18; Gal. 6:6; Gen. 45:11; Gen. 47:12. [11] 1 Pet. 2:18; Prov. 23:22; Gen. 9:23. [12] Psa. 127:3-5; Prov. 31:23.

**Question 128: What are the sins of inferiors against their superiors?**

**Answer:** The sins of inferiors against their superiors are, all neglect of the duties required toward them;[1] envying at,[2] contempt of,[3] and rebellion[4] against, their persons[5] and places,[6] in their lawful counsels,[7] commands, and corrections;[8] cursing, mocking,[9] and all such refractory and scandalous carriage, as proves a shame and dishonour to them and their government.[10]

[1] Matt. 15:4-6. [2] Num. 11:28-29. [3] 1 Sam. 8:7; Isa. 3:5. [4] 2 Sam. 15:1-12. [5] Exod. 21:15. [6] 1 Sam. 10:27. [7] 1 Sam. 2:25. [8] Deut. 21:18-21. [9] Prov. 30:11, 17. [10] Prov. 19:26.

**Question 129: What is required of superiors towards their inferiors?**

**Answer:** It is required of superiors, according to that power they receive from God, and that relation wherein they stand, to love,[1] pray for,[2] and bless their inferiors;[3] to instruct,[4] counsel, and admonish them;[5] countenancing,[6] commending,[7] and rewarding such as do well;[8] and discountenancing,[9] reproving, and chastising such as do ill;[10] protecting,[11] and providing for them all things necessary for soul[12] and body:[13] and by grave, wise, holy, and exemplary carriage, to procure glory to God,[14] honour to themselves,[15] and so to preserve that authority which God hath put upon them.[16]

[1] Col. 3:19; Titus 2:4. [2] 1 Sam. 12:23; Job 1:5. [3] 1 Kings 8:55-56; Heb. 7:7; Gen. 49:28; [4] Deut. 6:6-7. [5] Eph. 6:4. [6] 1 Pet. 3:7. [7] 1 Pet. 2:14; Rom. 13:3. [8] Esther 6:3. [9] Rom. 13:3-4. [10] Prov. 29:15; 1 Pet. 2:14. [11] Job 29:12-17; Isa. 1:10, 17. [12] Eph. 6:4. [13] 1 Tim. 5:8. [14] 1 Tim. 4:12; Titus 2:3-5. [15] 1 Kings 3:28. [16] Titus 2:15.

**Question 130: What are the sins of superiors?**

**Answer:** The sins of superiors are, besides the neglect of the duties required of them,[1] and inordinate seeking of themselves,[2] their own glory,[3] ease, profit, or pleasure;[4] commanding things unlawful,[5] or not in the power of inferiors to perform;[6] counselling,[7] encouraging,[8] or favouring them in that which is evil;[9] dissuading, discouraging, or discountenancing them in that which is good;[10] correcting them unduly;[11] careless exposing, or leaving them to wrong, temptation, and danger;[12] provoking them to wrath;[13] or any way dishonouring themselves, or lessening their authority, by an unjust, indiscreet, rigorous, or remiss behaviour.[14]

[1] Ezek. 34:2-4. [2] Phil. 2:21. [3] John 5:44; John 7:18. [4] Isa. 56:10-11; Deut. 17:17. [5] Dan. 3:4-6; Acts 4:17-18. [6] Exod. 5:10-18; Matt. 23:2, 4. [7] Matt. 14:8 compared with Mark 6:24. [8] 2 Sam. 13:28. [9] 1 Sam. 3:13. [10] John 7:46-49; Col. 3:21; Exod. 5:17. [11] 1 Pet. 2:18-20; Heb. 12:10; Deut. 25:3. [12] Gen. 38:11, 26; Acts 18:17. [13] Eph. 6:4. [14] Gen. 9:21; 1 Kings 12:13-16; 1 Kings 1:6; 1 Sam. 2:29-31.

### Question 131: What are the duties of equals?

**Answer:** The duties of equals are, to regard the dignity and worth of each other,[1] in giving honour to go one before another;[2] and to rejoice in each others' gifts and advancement, as their own.[3]

[1] 1 Pet. 2:17. [2] Rom. 12:10. [3] Rom. 12:15-16; Phil. 2:3-4.

### Question 132: What are the sins of equals?

**Answer:** The sins of equals are, besides the neglect of the duties required,[1] the undervaluing of the worth,[2] envying the gifts,[3] grieving at the advancement or prosperity one of another;[4] and usurping pre-eminence one over another.[5]

[1] Rom. 13:8. [2] 2 Tim. 3:3. [3] Acts 7:9; Gal. 5:26. [4] Num. 12:2; Esther 6:12-13. [5] 3 John 9; Luke 22:24.

### Question 133: What is the reason annexed to the fifth commandment, the more to enforce it?

**Answer:** The reason annexed to the fifth commandment, in these words, *That thy days may be long upon the land which the Lord thy God giveth thee,*[1] is an express promise of long life and prosperity, as far as it shall serve for God's glory and their own good, to all such as keep this commandment.[2]

[1] Exod. 20:12. [2] Deut. 5:16; 1 Kings 8:25; Eph. 6:2-3.

### Question 134: Which is the sixth commandment?

**Answer:** The sixth commandment is, *Thou shalt not kill.*[1]

[1] Exod. 20:13.

### Question 135: What are the duties required in the sixth commandment?

**Answer:** The duties required in the sixth commandment are, all careful studies, and lawful endeavours, to preserve the life of ourselves[1] and others[2] by resisting all thoughts and purposes,[3] subduing all passions,[4] and avoiding all occasions,[5] temptations,[6] and practices, which tend to the unjust taking away the life of any;[7] by just defence thereof against violence,[8] patient bearing of the hand of God,[9] quietness of mind,[10] cheerfulness of spirit;[11] a sober use of meat,[12] drink,[13] physic,[14] sleep,[15] labour,[16] and recreations;[17] by charitable thoughts,[18] love,[19] compassion,[20] meekness, gentleness, kindness;[21] peaceable,[22] mild and courteous speeches and behaviour;[23] forbearance, readiness to be reconciled, patient bearing and forgiving of injuries, and requiting good for evil;[24] comforting and succouring the distressed and protecting and defending the innocent.[25]

[1] Eph. 5:28-29. [2] 1 Kings 18:4. [3] Jer. 26:15-16; Acts 23:12, 16-17, 21, 27. [4] Eph. 4:26-27. [5] 2 Sam. 2:22; Deut. 22:8. [6] Matt. 4:6-7; Prov. 1:10, 11, 15-16. [7] 1 Sam. 24:12; 1 Sam. 26:9-11; Gen. 37:21-22. [8] Psa. 82:4; Prov. 24:11-12; 1 Sam. 14:45. [9] James 5:7-11; Heb. 12:9. [10] 1 Thess. 4:11; 1 Pet. 3:3-4; Psa. 37:8-11. [11] Prov. 17:22. [12] Prov. 25:16, 27. [13] 1 Tim. 5:23. [14] Isa. 38:21. [15] Psa. 127:2. [16] Eccles. 5:12; 2 Thess. 3:10, 12 ; Prov. 16:26. [17] Eccles. 3:4, 11. [18] 1 Sam. 19:4-5; 1 Sam. 22:13-14. [19] Rom. 13:10. [20] Luke 10:33-34. [21] Col. 3:12-13. [22] James 3:17. [23] 1 Pet. 3:8-11; Prov. 15:1; Judg. 8:1-3. [24] Matt. 5:24; Eph. 4:2, 32; Rom. 12:17, 20-21. [25] 1 Thess. 5:14; Job 31:19-20; Matt. 25:35-36; Prov. 31:8-9.


### Question 136: What are the sins forbidden in the sixth commandment?

**Answer:** The sins forbidden in the sixth commandment are, all taking away the life of ourselves,[1] or of others,[2] except in case of public justice,[3] lawful war,[4] or necessary defence;[5] the neglecting or withdrawing the lawful and necessary means of preservation of life;[6] sinful anger,[7] hatred,[8] envy,[9] desire of revenge;[10] all excessive passions,[11] distracting cares;[12] immoderate use of meat, drink,[13] labour,[14] and recreations;[15] provoking words,[16] oppression,[17] quarrelling,[18] striking, wounding,[19] and whatsoever else tends to the destruction of the life of any.[20]

[1] Acts 16:28. [2] Gen. 9:6. [3] Num. 35:31, 33. [4] Jer. 48:10; Deut. 20. [5] Exod. 22:2-3. [6] Matt. 25:42-43; James 2:15-16; Eccles. 6:1-2. [7] Matt. 5:22. [8] 1 John 3:15; Lev. 19:17. [9] Prov. 14:30. [10] Rom. 12:19. [11] Eph. 4:31. [12] Matt. 6:31, 34. [13] Luke 21:34; Rom. 13:13. [14] Eccles. 12:12; Eccles. 2:22-23. [15] Isa. 5:12. [16] Prov. 15:1; Prov. 12:18. [17] Ezek. 18:18; Exod. 1:14. [18] Gal. 5:15; Prov. 23:29. [19] Num. 35:16-18, 21. [20] Exod. 21:18-36.


### Question 137: Which is the seventh commandment?

**Answer:** The seventh commandment is, *Thou shalt not commit adultery.*[1]

[1] Exod. 20:14.

**Question 138: What are the duties required in the seventh commandment?**

**Answer:** The duties required in the seventh commandment are, chastity in body, mind, affections,[1] words,[2] and behaviour;[3] and the preservation of it in ourselves and others;[4] watchfulness over the eyes and all the senses;[5] temperance,[6] keeping of chaste company,[7] modesty in apparel;[8] marriage by those that have not the gift of continency,[9] conjugal love,[10] and cohabitation;[11] diligent labour in our callings;[12] shunning all occasions of uncleanness, and resisting temptations thereunto.[13]

[1] 1 Thess. 4:4; Job 31:1; 1 Cor. 7:34. [2] Col. 4:6. [3] 1 Pet. 3:2. [4] 1 Cor. 7:2, 35-36. [5] Job 31:1. [6] Acts 24:24-25. [7] Prov. 2:16-20. [8] 1 Tim. 2:9. [9] 1 Cor. 7:2, 9. [10] Prov. 5:19-20. [11] 1 Pet. 3:7. [12] Prov. 31:11, 27-28. [13] Prov. 5:8; Gen. 39:8-10.

**Question 139: What are the sins forbidden in the seventh commandment?**

**Answer:** The sins forbidden in the seventh commandment, besides the neglect of the duties required,[1] are, adultery, fornication,[2] rape, incest,[3] sodomy, and all unnatural lusts;[4] all unclean imaginations, thoughts, purposes, and affections;[5] all corrupt or filthy communications, or listening thereunto;[6] wanton looks,[7] impudent or light behaviour, immodest apparel;[8] prohibiting of lawful,[9] and dispensing with unlawful marriages;[10] allowing, tolerating, keeping of stews, and resorting to them;[11] entangling vows of single life,[12] undue delay of marriage;[13] having more wives or husbands than one at the same time;[14] unjust divorce,[15] or desertion;[16] idleness, gluttony, drunkenness,[17] unchaste company;[18] lascivious songs, books, pictures, dancings, stage plays;[19] and all other provocations to, or acts of uncleanness, either in ourselves or others.[20]

[1] Prov. 5:7. [2] Heb. 13:4; Gal. 5:19. [3] 2 Sam. 13:14; 1 Cor. 5:1. [4] Rom. 1:24, 26-27; Lev. 20:15-16. [5] Matt. 5:28; Matt. 15:19; Col. 3:5. [6] Eph. 5:3-4; Prov. 7:5, 21-22. [7] Isa. 3:16; 2 Pet. 2:14. [8] Prov. 7:10, 13. [9] 1 Tim. 4:3. [10] Lev. 18:1-21; Mark 6:18; Mal. 2:11-12. [11] 1 Kings 15:12; 2 Kings 23:7; Deut. 23:17-18; Lev. 19:29; Jer. 5:7; Prov. 7:24-27. [12] Matt. 19:10-11. [13] 1 Cor. 7:7-9; Gen. 38:26. [14] Mal. 2:14-15; Matt. 19:5. [15] Mal. 2:16; Matt. 5:32. [16] 1 Cor. 7:12-13. [17] Ezek. 16:49; Prov. 23:30-33. [18] Gen. 39:10; Prov. 5:8. [19] Eph. 5:4; Ezek. 23:14-16; Isa. 23:15-17; Isa. 3:16; Mark 6:22; Rom. 13:13; 1 Pet. 4:3. [20] 2 Kings 9:30 compared with Jer. 4:30. And with Ezek. 23:40.

**Question 140: Which is the eighth commandment?**
**Answer:** The eighth commandment is, *Thou shalt not steal.*[1]

[1] Exod. 20:15.

**Question 141: What are the duties required in the eighth commandment?**
**Answer:** The duties required in the eighth commandment are, truth, faithfulness, and justice in contracts and commerce between man and man;[1] rendering to everyone his due;[2] restitution of goods unlawfully detained from the right owners thereof;[3] giving and lending freely, according to our abilities, and the necessities of others;[4] moderation of our judgments, wills, and affections concerning worldly goods;[5] a provident care and study to get,[6] keep, use, and dispose these things which are necessary and convenient for the sustentation of our nature, and suitable to our condition;[7] a lawful calling,[8] and diligence in it;[9] frugality;[10] avoiding unnecessary lawsuits,[11] and suretiship, or other like engagements;[12] and an endeavour, by all just and lawful means, to procure, preserve, and further the wealth and outward estate of others, as well as our own.[13]

[1] Psa. 15:2, 4; Zech. 7:4, 10; Zech. 8:16-17. [2] Rom. 13:7. [3] Lev. 6:2-5 compared with Luke 19:8. [4] Luke 6:30, 38; 1 John 3:17; Eph. 4:28; Gal. 6:10. [5] 1 Tim. 6:6-9; Gal. 6:14. [6] 1 Tim. 5:8. [7] Prov. 27:23-27; Eccles. 2:24; Eccles. 3:12-13; 1 Tim. 6:17-18; Isa. 38:1; Matt. 11:8. [8] 1 Cor. 7:20; Gen. 2:15; Gen. 3:19. [9] Eph. 4:28; Prov. 10:4. [10] John 6:12; Prov. 21:20. [11] 1 Cor. 6:1-9. [12] Prov. 6:1-6; Prov. 11:15. [13] Lev. 25:35; Deut. 22:1-4; Exod. 23:4-5; Gen. 47:14, 20; Phil. 2:4; Matt. 22:39.

**Question 142: What are the sins forbidden in the eighth commandment?**
**Answer:** The sins forbidden in the eighth commandment, besides the neglect of the duties required,[1] are, theft,[2] robbery,[3] man-stealing,[4] and receiving any thing that is stolen;[5] fraudulent dealing,[6] false weights and measures,[7] removing landmarks,[8] injustice and unfaithfulness in contracts between man and man,[9] or in matters of trust;[10] oppression,[11] extortion,[12] usury,[13] bribery,[14] vexatious lawsuits,[15] unjust inclosures and depopulations;[16] ingrossing commodities to enhance the price;[17] unlawful callings,[18] and all other unjust or sinful ways of taking or withholding from our neighbour what belongs to him, or of enriching ourselves;[19] covetousness;[20] inordinate prizing and affecting worldly goods;[21] distrustful and distracting cares and studies in getting, keeping, and using them;[22] envying at the prosperity of others;[23] as likewise idleness,[24] prodigality, wasteful gaming; and all

other ways whereby we do unduly prejudice our own outward estate,[25] and defrauding ourselves of the due use and comfort of that estate which God hath given us.[26]

[1] James 2:15-16; 1 John 3:17. [2] Eph. 4:28. [3] Psa. 62:10. [4] 1 Tim. 1:10. [5] Prov. 29:24; Psa. 50:18. [6] 1 Thess. 4:6. [7] Prov. 11:1; Prov. 20:10. [8] Deut. 19:14; Prov. 23:10. [9] Amos 8:5; Psa. 37:21. [10] Luke 16:10-12. [11] Ezek. 22:29; Lev. 25:17. [12] Matt. 23:25; Ezek. 22:12. [13] Psa. 15:5. [14] Job 15:34. [15] 1 Cor. 6:6-8; Prov. 3:29-30. [16] Isa. 5:8; Mic. 2:2. [17] Prov. 11:26. [18] Acts 19:19, 24-25. [19] Job 20:19; James 5:4; Prov. 21:6. [20] Luke 12:15. [21] 1 Tim. 6:5; Col. 3:2; Prov. 23:5; Psa. 62:10. [22] Matt. 6:25, 31, 34; Eccles. 5:12. [23] Psa. 73:3; Psa. 37:1, 7. [24] 2 Thess. 3:11; Prov. 18:9. [25] Prov. 21:17 ; Prov. 23:20-21; Prov. 28:19. [26] Eccles. 4:8; Eccles. 6:2; 1 Tim. 5:8.

## Question 143: Which is the ninth commandment?

**Answer:** The ninth commandment is, *Thou shalt not bear false witness against thy neighbour.*[1]

[1] Exod. 20:16.

## Question 144: What are the duties required in the ninth commandment?

**Answer:** The duties required in the ninth commandment are, the preserving and promoting of truth between man and man,[1] and the good name of our neighbour, as well as our own;[2] appearing and standing for the truth;[3] and from the heart,[4] sincerely,[5] freely,[6] clearly,[7] and fully,[8] speaking the truth, and only the truth, in matters of judgment and justice,[9] and in all other things whatsoever;[10] a charitable esteem of our neighbours;[11] loving, desiring, and rejoicing in their good name;[12] sorrowing for,[13] and covering of their infirmities;[14] freely acknowledging of their gifts and graces,[15] defending their innocency;[16] a ready receiving of a good report,[17] and unwillingness to admit of an evil report,[18] concerning them; discouraging tale-bearers,[19] flatterers,[20] and slanderers;[21] love and care of our own good name, and defending it when need requireth;[22] keeping of lawful promises;[23] studying and practicing of whatsoever things are true, honest, lovely, and of good report.[24]

[1] Zech. 8:16. [2] 3 John 12. [3] Prov. 31:8-9. [4] Psa. 15:2. [5] 2 Chron. 19:9. [6] 1 Sam. 19:4-5. [7] Josh. 7:19. [8] 2 Sam. 14:18-20. [9] Lev. 19:15; Prov. 14:5, 25. [10] 2 Cor. 1:17-18; Eph. 4:25. [11] Heb. 6:9; 1 Cor. 13:7. [12] Rom. 1:8; 2 John 4; 3 John 3-4. [13] 2 Cor. 2:4; 2 Cor. 12:21. [14] Prov. 17:9; 1 Pet. 4:8. [15] 1 Cor. 1:4-5, 7; 2 Tim. 1:4-5. [16] 1 Sam. 22:14. [17] 1 Cor. 13:6-7. [18] Psa. 15:3. [19] Prov. 25:23. [20] Prov. 26:24-25. [21] Psa. 101:5. [22] Prov. 22:1 ; John 8:49. [23] Psa. 15:4. [24] Phil. 4:8.

**Question 145: What are the sins forbidden in the ninth commandment?**

**Answer:** The sins forbidden in the ninth commandment are, all prejudicing the truth, and the good name of our neighbours, as well as our own,[1] especially in public judicature;[2] giving false evidence,[3] suborning false witnesses,[4] wittingly appearing and pleading for an evil cause, out-facing and over-bearing the truth;[5] passing unjust sentence,[6] calling evil good, and good evil; rewarding the wicked according to the work of the righteous, and the righteous according to the work of the wicked;[7] forgery,[8] concealing the truth, undue silence in a just cause,[9] and holding our peace when iniquity calleth for either a reproof from ourselves,[10] or complaint to others;[11] speaking the truth unseasonably,[12] or maliciously to a wrong end,[13] or perverting it to a wrong meaning,[14] or in doubtful and equivocal expressions, to the prejudice of truth or justice;[15] speaking untruth,[16] lying,[17] slandering,[18] backbiting,[19] detracting,[20] tale-bearing,[21] whispering,[22] scoffing,[23] reviling,[24] rash,[25] harsh,[26] and partial censuring;[27] misconstructing intentions, words, and actions;[28] flattering,[29] vain-glorious boasting,[30] thinking or speaking too highly or too meanly of ourselves or others;[31] denying the gifts and graces of God;[32] aggravating smaller faults;[33] hiding, excusing, or extenuating of sins, when called to a free confession;[34] unnecessary discovering of infirmities;[35] raising false rumours,[36] receiving and countenancing evil reports,[37] and stopping our ears against just defence;[38] evil suspicion;[39] envying or grieving at the deserved credit of any,[40] endeavouring or desiring to impair it,[41] rejoicing in their disgrace and infamy;[42] scornful contempt,[43] fond admiration;[44] breach of lawful promises;[45] neglecting such things as are of good report,[46] and practising, or not avoiding ourselves, or not hindering what we can in others, such things as procure an ill name.[47]

[1] 1 Sam. 17:28; 2 Sam. 16:3; 2 Sam. 1:9-10, 15-16. [2] Lev. 19:15 ; Hab. 1:4. [3] Prov. 19:5; Prov. 6:16, 19. [4] Acts 6:13. [5] Jer. 9:3, 5; Acts 24:2, 5; Psa. 12:3-4; Psa. 52:1-4. [6] Prov. 17:15; 1 Kings 21:9-14. [7] Isa. 5:23. [8] Psa. 119:69; Luke 19:8; Luke 16:5-7. [9] Lev. 5:1; Deut. 13:8; Acts 5:3, 8-9; 2 Tim. 4:16. [10] 1 Kings 1:6; Lev. 19:17. [11] Isa. 59:4. [12] Prov. 29:11. [13] 1 Sam. 22:9-10 compared with Psa. 52 [title, *A Psalm of David, when Doeg the Edomite came and told Saul,* and said unto him, David is come to the house of Ahimelech] verses 1-5. [14] Psa. 56:5; John 2:19 compared with Matt. 26:60-61. [15] Gen. 3:5; Gen. 26:7, 9. [16] Isa. 59:13. [17] Lev. 19:11; Col. 3:9. [18] Psa. 50:20. [19] Psa. 15:3. [20] James 4:11; Jer. 38:4. [21] Lev. 19:16. [22] Rom. 1:29-30. [23] Gen. 21:9 compared with Gal. 4:29. [24] 1 Cor. 6:10. [25] Matt. 7:1. [26] Acts 28:4. [27] Gen. 38:24. Rom. 2:1. [28] Neh. 6:6-8; Rom. 3:8; Psa. 69:10; 1 Sam. 1:13-15; 2 Sam. 10:3. [29] Psa. 12:2-3. [30] 2 Tim. 3:2. [31] Luke 18:9, 11; Rom. 12:16; 1 Cor. 4:6; Acts 12:22; Exod. 4:10-14. [32] Job 27:5-6;

Job 4:6. [33] Matt. 7:3-5. [34] Prov. 28:13; Prov. 30:20; Gen. 3:12-13; Jer. 2:35; 2 Kings 5:25; Gen. 4:9. [35] Gen. 9:22;. Prov. 25:9-10. [36] Exod. 23:1. [37] Prov. 29:12. [38] Acts 7:56-57; Job 31:13-14. [39] 1 Cor. 13:5; 1 Tim. 6:4. [40] Num. 11:29; Matt. 21:15. [41] Ezra 4:12-13. [42] Jer. 48:27. [43] Psa. 35:15-16, 21; Matt. 27:28-29. [44] Jude 16; Acts 12:22. [45] Rom. 1:31; 2 Tim. 3:3. [46] 1 Sam. 2:24. [47] 2 Sam. 13:12-13; Prov. 5:8-9; Prov. 6:33.

## Question 146: Which is the tenth commandment?

**Answer:** The tenth commandment is, *Thou shalt not covet thy neighbour's house, thou shall not covet they neighbour's wife, nor his man-servant, nor his maid-servant, nor his ox, nor his ass, nor any thing that is thy neighbour's.*[1]

[1] Exod. 20:17.

## Question 147: What are the duties required in the tenth commandment?

**Answer:** The duties required in the tenth commandment are, such a full contentment with our own condition,[1] and such a charitable frame of the whole soul toward our neighbour, as that all our inward motions and affections touching him, tend unto, and further all that good which is his.[2]

[1] Heb. 13:5; 1 Tim. 6:6. [2] Job 31:29; Rom. 12:15; Psa. 122:7-9; 1 Tim. 1:5; Esther 10:3; 1 Cor. 13:4-7.

## Question 148: What are the sins forbidden in the tenth commandment?

**Answer:** The sins forbidden in the tenth commandment are, discontentment with our own estate;[1] envying[2] and grieving at the good of our neighbour,[3] together with all inordinate motions and affections to anything that is his.[4]

[1] 1 Kings 21:4; Esther 5:13; 1 Cor. 10:10. [2] Gal. 5:26; James 3:14, 16. [3] Psa. 112:9-10; Neh. 2:10. [4] Rom. 7:7-8; Rom. 13:9; Col. 3:5; Deut. 5:21.

## Question 149: Is any man able perfectly to keep the commandments of God?

**Answer:** No man is able, either of himself,[1] or by any grace received in this life, perfectly to keep the commandments of God;[2] but doth daily break them in thought,[3] word, and deed.[4]

[1] James 3:2; John 15:5; Rom. 8:3. [2] Eccles. 7:20; 1 John 1:8, 10; Gal. 5:17; Rom. 7:18-19. [3] Gen. 6:5; Gen. 8:21. [4] Rom. 3:9-19; James 3:2-13.

**Question 150: Are all transgressions of the law of God equally heinous in themselves, and in the sight of God?**

**Answer:** All transgressions of the law of God are not equally heinous; but some sins in themselves, and by reason of several aggravations, are more heinous in the sight of God than others.[1]

[1] John 19:11; Ezek. 8:6, 13, 15; 1 John 5:16; Psa. 78:17, 32, 56.


**Question 151: What are those aggravations that make some sins more heinous than others?**

**Answer:** Sins receive their aggravations,

**1.** From the persons offending;[1] if they be of riper age,[2] greater experience or grace,[3] eminent for profession,[4] gifts,[5] place,[6] office,[7] guides to others,[8] and whose example is likely to be followed by others.[9]

[1] Jer. 2:8. [2] Job 32:7, 9; Eccles. 4:13. [3] 1 Kings 11:4, 9. [4] 2 Sam. 12:14; 1 Cor. 5:1. [5] James 4:17; Luke 12:47-48. [6] Jer. 5:4-5. [7] 2 Sam. 12:7-9; Ezek. 8:11-12. [8] Rom. 2:17-24. [9] Gal. 2:11-14.

**2.** From the parties offended:[1] if immediately against God,[2] his attributes,[3] and worship;[4] against Christ, and his grace;[5] the Holy Spirit,[6] his witness,[7] and workings;[8] against superiors, men of eminency,[9] and such as we stand especially related and engaged unto;[10] against any of the saints,[11] particularly weak brethren,[12] the souls of them, or any other,[13] and the common good of all or many.[14]

[1] Matt. 21:38-39. [2] 1 Sam. 2:25; Acts 5:4; Psa. 51:4. [3] Rom. 2:4. [4] Mal. 1:8, 14. [5] Heb. 2:2-3; Heb. 12:25. [6] Heb. 10:29; Matt. 12:31-32. [7] Eph. 4:30. [8] Heb. 6:4-6. [9] Jude 8; Num. 12:8-9; Isa. 3:5. [10] Prov. 30:17; 2 Cor. 12:15; Psa. 55:12-15. [11] Zeph. 2:8, 10-11; Matt. 18:6; 1 Cor. 6:8; Rev. 17:6. [12] 1 Cor. 8:11-12; Rom. 14:13, 15, 21. [13] Ezek. 13:19; 1 Cor. 8:12; Rev. 18:12-13; Matt. 23:15. [14] 1 Thess. 2:15-16; Josh. 22:20.

**3.** From the nature and quality of the offence:[1] if it be against the express letter of the law,[2] break many commandments, contain in it many sins:[3] if not only conceived in the heart, but breaks forth in words and actions,[4] scandalize others,[5] and admit of no reparation:[6] if against means,[7] mercies,[8] judgments,[9] light of nature,[10] conviction of conscience,[11] public or private admonition,[12] censures of the church,[13] civil punishments;[14] and our prayers, purposes, promises,[15] vows,[16] covenants,[17] and engagements to God or men:[18] if done deliberately,[19] wilfully,[20] presumptuously,[21] impudently,[22] boastingly,[23] maliciously,[24] frequently,[25] obstinately,[26] with delight,[27] continuance,[28] or relapsing after repentance.[29]

[1] Prov. 6:30-35. [2] Ezra 9:10-12; 1 Kings 11:9-10. [3] Col. 3:5; 1 Tim. 6:10; Prov. 5:8-12; Prov. 6:32-33; Josh. 7:21. [4] James 1:14-15; Matt. 5:22; Mic. 2:1. [5] Matt. 18:7; Rom. 2:23-24. [6] Deut. 22:22 compared with Deut. 22:28-29; Prov. 6:32-35. [7] Matt. 11:21-24; John 15:22. [8] Isa. 1:3; Deut. 32:6. [9] Amos 4:8-11; Jer. 5:3. [10] Rom. 1:26-27. [11] Rom. 1:32; Dan. 5:22; Titus 3:10-11. [12] Prov. 29:1. [13] Titus 3:10; Matt. 18:17. [14] Prov. 27:22; Prov. 23:35. [15] Psa. 78:34-37; Jer. 2:20; Jer. 42:5-6, 20-21. [16] Eccles. 5:4-6; Prov. 20:25. [17] Lev. 26:25. [18] Prov. 2:17; Ezek. 17:18-19. [19] Psa. 36:4. [20] Jer. 6:16. [21] Num. 15:30; Exod. 21:14. [22] Jer. 3:3; Prov. 7:13. [23] Psa. 52:1. [24] 3 John 10. [25] Num. 14:22. [26] Zech. 7:11-12. [27] Prov. 2:14. [28] Isa. 57:17. [29] Jer. 34:8-11; 2 Pet. 2:20-22.

**4.** From circumstances of time[1] and place:[2] if on the Lord's day,[3] or other times of divine worship;[4] or immediately before[5] or after these,[6] or other helps to prevent or remedy such miscarriages:[7] if in public, or in the presence of others, who are thereby likely to be provoked or defiled.[8]

[1] 2 Kings 5:26. [2] Jer. 7:10; Isa. 26:10. [3] Ezek. 23:37-39. [4] Isa. 58:3-5; Num. 25:6-7. [5] 1 Cor. 11:20-21. [6] Jer. 7:8-10; Prov. 7:14-15; John 13:27, 30. [7] Ezra 9:13-14. [8] 2 Sam. 16:22; 1 Sam. 2:22-24.

### Question 152: What doth every sin deserve at the hands of God?

**Answer:** Every sin, even the least, being against the sovereignty,[1] goodness,[2] and holiness of God,[3] and against his righteous law,[4] deserveth his wrath and curse,[5] both in this life,[6] and that which is to come;[7] and cannot be expiated but by the blood of Christ.[8]

[1] James 2:10-11. [2] Exod. 20:1-2. [3] Hab. 1:13; Lev. 10:3; Lev. 11:44-45. [4] 1 John 3:4; Rom. 7:12. [5] Eph. 5:6; Gal. 3:10. [6] Lam. 3:39; Deut. 28:15-68. [7] Matt. 25:41. [8] Heb. 9:22; 1 Pet. 1:18-19.

### Question 153: What doth God require of us, that we may escape his wrath and curse due to us by reason of the transgression of the law?

**Answer:** That we may escape the wrath and curse of God due to us by reason of the transgression of the law, he requireth of us repentance toward God, and faith toward our Lord Jesus Christ,[1] and the diligent use of the outward means whereby Christ communicates to us the benefits of his mediation.[2]

[1] Acts 20:21; Matt. 3:7-8; Luke 13:3, 5; Acts 16:30-31; John 3:16, 18. [2] Prov. 2:1-5; Prov. 8:33-36.

**Question 154: What are the outward means whereby Christ communicates to us the benefits of his mediation?**

**Answer:** The outward and ordinary means whereby Christ communicates to his church the benefits of his mediation, are all his ordinances; especially the word, sacraments, and prayer; all which are made effectual to the elect for their salvation.[1]

[1] Matt. 28:19-20; Acts 2:42, 46-47.


**Question 155: How is the word made effectual to salvation?**

**Answer:** The Spirit of God maketh the reading, but especially the preaching of the word, an effectual means of enlightening,[1] convincing, and humbling sinners;[2] of driving them out of themselves, and drawing them unto Christ;[3] of conforming them to his image,[4] and subduing them to his will;[5] of strengthening them against temptations and corruptions;[6] of building them up in grace,[7] and establishing their hearts in holiness and comfort through faith unto salvation.[8]

[1] Neh. 8:8; Acts 26:18; Psa. 19:8. [2] 1 Cor. 14:24-25; 2 Chron. 34:18-19, 26-28. [3] Acts 2:37, 41; Acts 8:27-39. [4] 2 Cor. 3:18. [5] 2 Cor. 10:4-6; Rom. 6:17. [6] Matt. 4:4, 7, 10; Eph. 6:16-17; Psa. 19:11; 1 Cor. 10:11. [7] Acts 20:32; 2 Tim. 3:15-17. [8] Rom. 16:25; 1 Thess. 3:2, 10-11, 13; Rom. 15:4; Rom. 10:13-17; Rom. 1:16.


**Question 156: Is the word of God to be read by all?**

**Answer:** Although all are not to be permitted to read the word publicly to the congregation,[1] yet all sorts of people are bound to read it apart by themselves,[2] and with their families:[3] to which end, the Holy Scriptures are to be translated out of the original into vulgar languages.[4]

[1] Deut. 31:9, 11-13; Neh. 8:2-3; Neh. 9:3-5. [2] Deut. 17:19; Rev. 1:3; John 5:39; Isa. 34:16. [3] Deut. 6:6-9; Gen. 18:17, 19; Psa. 78:5-7. [4] 1 Cor. 14:6, 9, 11-12, 15-16, 24, 27-28.


**Question 157: How is the word of God to be read?**

**Answer:** The Holy Scriptures are to be read with an high and reverent esteem of them;[1] with a firm persuasion that they are the very word of God,[2] and that he only can enable us to understand them;[3] with desire to know, believe, and obey the will of God revealed in them;[4] with diligence,[5] and attention to the matter and scope of them;[6] with meditation,[7] application,[8] self-denial,[9] and prayer.[10]

[1] Psa. 19:10; Neh. 8:3-10; Exod. 24:7; 2 Chron. 34:27; Isa. 66:2. [2] 2 Pet. 1:19-21. [3] Luke 24:45; 2 Cor. 3:13-16. [4] Deut. 17:10, 20. [5] Acts 17:11. [6] Acts 8:30, 34; Luke 10:26-28. [7] Psa. 1:2; Psa. 119:97. [8] 2 Chron. 34:21. [9] Prov. 3:5; Deut. 33:3. [10] Prov. 2:1-6; Psa. 119:18; Neh. 8:6, 8.

### Question 158: By whom is the word of God to be preached?

**Answer:** The word of God is to be preached only by such as are sufficiently gifted,[1] and also duly approved and called to that office.[2]

[1] 1 Tim. 3:2, 6; Eph. 4:8-11; Hos. 4:6; Mal. 2:7; 2 Cor. 3:6. [2] Jer. 14:15; Rom. 10:15; Heb. 5:4; 1 Cor. 12:28-29; 1 Tim. 3:10; 1 Tim. 4:14; 1 Tim. 5:22.

### Question 159: How is the word of God to be preached by those that are called thereunto?

**Answer:** They that are called to labour in the ministry of the word, are to preach sound doctrine,[1] diligently,[2] in season and out of season;[3] plainly,[4] not in the enticing words of man's wisdom, but in demonstration of the Spirit, and of power;[5] faithfully,[6] making known the whole counsel of God;[7] wisely,[8] applying themselves to the necessities and capacities of the hearers;[9] zealously,[10] with fervent love to God[11] and the souls of his people;[12] sincerely,[13] aiming at his glory,[14] and their conversion,[15] edification,[16] and salvation.[17]

[1] Titus 2:1, 8. [2] Acts 18:25. [3] 2 Tim. 4:2. [4] 1 Cor. 14:19. [5] 1 Cor. 2:4. [6] Jer. 23:28; 1 Cor. 4:1-2. [7] Acts 20:27. [8] Col. 1:28; 2 Tim. 2:15. [9] 1 Cor. 3:2; Heb. 5:12-14; Luke 12:42. [10] Acts 18:25. [11] 2 Cor. 5:13-14; Phil. 1:15-17. [12] Col. 4:12; 2 Cor. 12:15. [13] 2 Cor. 2:17; 2 Cor. 4:2. [14] 1 Thess. 2:4-6; John 7:18. [15] 1 Cor. 9:19-22. [16] 2 Cor. 12:19; Eph. 4:12. [17] 1 Tim. 4:16; Acts 26:16-18.

### Question 160: What is required of those that hear the word preached?

**Answer:** It is required of those that hear the word preached, that they attend upon it with diligence,[1] preparation,[2] and prayer;[3] examine what they hear by the Scriptures;[4] receive the truth with faith,[5] love,[6] meekness,[7] and readiness of mind,[8] as the word of God;[9] meditate,[10] and confer of it;[11] hide it in their hearts,[12] and bring forth the fruit of it in their lives.[13]

[1] Prov. 8:34. [2] 1 Pet. 2:1-2; Luke 8:18. [3] Psa. 119:18; Eph. 6:18-19. [4] Acts 17:11. [5] Heb. 4:2. [6] 2 Thess. 2:10. [7] James 1:21. [8] Acts 17:11. [9] 1 Thess. 2:13. [10] Luke 9:44; Heb. 2:1. [11] Luke 24:14; Deut. 6:6-7. [12] Prov. 2:1; Psa. 119:11. [13] Luke 8:15; James 1:25.

**Question 161: How do the sacraments become effectual means of salvation?**

**Answer:** The sacraments become effectual means of salvation, not by any power in themselves, or any virtue derived from the piety or intention of him by whom they are administered, but only by the working of the Holy Ghost, and the blessing of Christ, by whom they are instituted.[1]

[1] 1 Pet. 3:21; Acts 8:13 compared with Acts 8:23; 1 Cor. 3:6-7; 1 Cor. 12:13.


**Question 162: What is a sacrament?**

**Answer:** A sacrament is an holy ordinance instituted by Christ in his church,[1] to signify, seal, and exhibit[2] unto those that are within the covenant of grace,[3] the benefits of his mediation;[4] to strengthen and increase their faith, and all other graces;[5] to oblige them to obedience;[6] to testify and cherish their love and communion one with another;[7] and to distinguish them from those that are without.[8]

[1] Gen. 17:7, 10; Exod. 12; Matt. 28:19; Matt. 26:26-28. [2] Rom. 4:11; 1 Cor. 11:24-25. [3] Rom. 15:8; Exod. 12:48. [4] Acts 2:38; 1 Cor. 10:16. [5] Rom. 4:11; Gal. 3:27. [6] Rom. 6:3-4; 1 Cor. 10:21. [7] Eph. 4:2-5; 1 Cor. 12:13. [8] Eph. 2:11-12; Gen. 34:14.


**Question 163: What are the parts of a sacrament?**

**Answer:** The parts of a sacrament are two; the one an outward and sensible sign, used according to Christ's own appointment; the other an inward and spiritual grace thereby signified.[1]

[1] Matt. 3:11; 1 Pet. 3:21; Rom. 2:28-29.


**Question 164: How many sacraments hath Christ instituted in his church under the New Testament?**

**Answer:** Under the New Testament Christ hath instituted in his church only two sacraments, baptism and the Lord's Supper.[1]

[1] Matt. 28:19; 1 Cor. 11:20, 23; Matt. 26:26-28.


**Question 165: What is baptism?**

**Answer:** Baptism is a sacrament of the New Testament, wherein Christ hath ordained the washing with water in the name of the Father, and of the Son, and of the Holy Ghost,[1] to be a sign and seal of ingrafting into himself,[2] of remission of sins by his blood,[3] and regeneration by his Spirit;[4] of adoption,[5] and resurrection unto everlasting life;[6] and whereby the parties baptized are solemnly admitted into the visible church,[7] and enter into an open and professed engagement to be wholly and only the Lord's.[8]

[1] Matt. 28:19. [2] Gal. 3:27. [3] Mark 1:4; Rev. 1:5. [4] Titus 3:5; Eph. 5:26. [5] Gal. 3:26-27. [6] 1 Cor. 15:29; Rom. 6:5. [7] 1 Cor. 12:13. [8] Rom. 6:4.

### Question 166: Unto whom is baptism to be administered?

**Answer:** Baptism is not to be administered to any that are out of the visible church, and so strangers from the covenant of promise, till they profess their faith in Christ, and obedience to him,[1] but infants descending from parents, either both, or but one of them, professing faith in Christ, and obedience to him, are in that respect within the covenant, and to be baptized.[2]

[1] Acts 8:36-37; Acts 2:38. [2] Gen. 17:7, 9 compared with Gal. 3:9, 14 and with Col. 2:11-12 and with Acts 2:38-39 and with Rom. 4:11-12; 1 Cor. 7:14; Matt. 28:19; Luke 18:15-16; Rom. 11:16.

### Question 167: How is our baptism to be improved by us?

**Answer:** The needful but much neglected duty of improving our baptism, is to be performed by us all our life long, especially in the time of temptation, and when we are present at the administration of it to others;[1] by serious and thankful consideration of the nature of it, and of the ends for which Christ instituted it, the privileges and benefits conferred and sealed thereby, and our solemn vow made therein;[2] by being humbled for our sinful defilement, our falling short of, and walking contrary to, the grace of baptism, and our engagements;[3] by growing up to assurance of pardon of sin, and of all other blessings sealed to us in that sacrament;[4] by drawing strength from the death and resurrection of Christ, into whom we are baptized, for the mortifying of sin, and quickening of grace;[5] and by endeavouring to live by faith,[6] to have our conversation in holiness and righteousness,[7] as those that have therein given up their names to Christ;[8] and to walk in brotherly love, as being baptized by the same Spirit into one body.[9]

[1] Col. 2:11-12; Rom. 6:4, 6, 11. [2] Rom. 6:3-5. [3] 1 Cor. 1:11-13; Rom. 6:2-3. [4] Rom. 4:11-12; 1 Pet. 3:21. [5] Rom. 6:3-5. [6] Gal. 3:26-27. [7] Rom. 6:22. [8] Acts 2:38. [9] 1 Cor. 12:13, 25-27.

### Question 168: What is the Lord's Supper?

**Answer:** The Lord's Supper is a sacrament of the New Testament,[1] wherein, by giving and receiving bread and wine according to the appointment of Jesus Christ, his death is showed forth; and they that worthily communicate feed upon his body and blood, to their spiritual nourishment and growth in grace;[2] have their union and communion with him confirmed;[3] testify and renew their thankfulness,[4] and engagement to God,[5] and their mutual love and fellowship each with other, as members of the same mystical body.[6]

[1] Luke 22:20. [2] Matt. 26:26-27; 1 Cor. 11:23-26. [3] 1 Cor. 10:16. [4] 1 Cor. 11:24. [5] 1 Cor. 10:14, 16, 21. [6] 1 Cor. 10:17.

### Question 169: How hath Christ appointed bread and wine to be given and received in the sacrament of the Lord's Supper?

**Answer:** Christ hath appointed the ministers of his word, in the administration of this sacrament of the Lord's Supper, to set apart the bread and wine from common use, by the word of institution, thanksgiving, and prayer; to take and break the bread, and to give both the bread and the wine to the communicants: who are, by the same appointment, to take and eat the bread, and to drink the wine, in thankful remembrance that the body of Christ was broken and given, and his blood shed, for them.[1]

[1] 1 Cor. 11:23-24; Matt. 26:26-28; Mark 14:22-24; Luke 22:19-20.

### Question 170: How do they that worthily communicate in the Lord's Supper feed upon the body and blood of Christ therein?

**Answer:** As the body and blood of Christ are not corporally or carnally present in, with, or under the bread and wine in the Lord's Supper,[1] and yet are spiritually present to the faith of the receiver, no less truly and really than the elements themselves are to their outward senses;[2] so they that worthily communicate in the sacrament of the Lord's Supper, do therein feed upon the body and blood of Christ, not after a corporal and carnal, but in a spiritual manner; yet truly and really,[3] while by faith they receive and apply unto themselves Christ crucified, and all the benefits of his death.[4]

[1] Acts 3:21. [2] Matt. 26:26, 28. [3] 1 Cor. 11:24-29. [4] 1 Cor. 10:16.

### Question 171: How are they that receive the sacrament of the Lord's Supper to prepare themselves before they come unto it?

**Answer:** They that receive the sacrament of the Lord's Supper are, before they come, to prepare themselves thereunto, by examining themselves[1] of their being in Christ,[2] of their sins and wants;[3] of the truth and measure of their knowledge,[4] faith,[5] repentance;[6] love to God and the brethren,[7] charity to all men,[8] forgiving those that have done them wrong;[9] of their desires after Christ,[10] and of their new obedience;[11] and by renewing the exercise of these graces,[12] by serious meditation,[13] and fervent prayer.[14]

[1] 1 Cor. 11:28. [2] 2 Cor. 13:5. [3] 1 Cor. 5:7 compared with Exod. 12:15. [4] 1 Cor. 11:29. [5] 2 Cor. 13:5; Matt. 26:28. [6] Zech. 12:10; 1 Cor. 11:31. [7] 1 Cor. 10:16-17; Acts 2:46-47. [8] 1 Cor. 5:8; 1 Cor. 11:18, 20. [9] Matt. 5:23-24. [10] Isa. 55:1; John 7:37. [11] 1 Cor. 5:7-8. [12] 1 Cor. 11:25-26, 28; Heb. 10:21-22, 24; Psa. 26:6. [13] 1 Cor. 11:24-25. [14] 2 Chron. 30:18-19; Matt. 26:26.

### Question 172: May one who doubteth of his being in Christ, or of his due preparation, come to the Lord's Supper?

**Answer:** One who doubteth of his being in Christ, or of his due preparation to the sacrament of the Lord's Supper, may have true interest in Christ, though he be not yet assured thereof;[1] and in God's account hath it, if he be duly affected with the apprehension of the want of it,[2] and unfeignedly desires to be found in Christ,[3] and to depart from iniquity:[4] in which case (because promises are made, and this sacrament is appointed, for the relief even of weak and doubting Christians)[5] he is to bewail his unbelief,[6] and labour to have his doubts resolved;[7] and, so doing, he may and ought to come to the Lord's Supper, that he may be further strengthened.[8]

[1] Isa. 50:10; 1 John 5:13; Psa. 88; Psa. 77:1-12; Jon. 2:4, 7. [2] Isa. 54:7-10; Matt. 5:3-4; Psa. 31:22; Psa. 73:13, 22-23. [3] Phil. 3:8-9; Psa. 10:17; Psa. 42:1-2, 5, 11. [4] 2 Tim. 2:19; Isa. 50:10; Psa. 66:18-20. [5] Isa. 40:11, 29, 31; Matt. 11:28; Matt. 12:20; Matt. 26:28. [6] Mark 9:24. [7] Acts 2:37; Acts 16:30. [8] Rom. 4:11; 1 Cor. 11:28.

### Question 173: May any who profess the faith, and desire to come to the Lord's Supper, be kept from it?

**Answer:** Such as are found to be ignorant or scandalous, notwithstanding their profession of the faith, and desire to come to the Lord's Supper, may and ought to be kept from that sacrament, by the power which Christ hath left in his church,[1] until they receive instruction, and manifest their reformation.[2]

[1] 1 Cor. 11:27-34 compared with Matt. 7:6. And with 1 Cor. 5. And with Jude 23 and with 1 Tim. 5:22. [2] 2 Cor. 2:7.

**Question 174: What is required of them that receive the sacrament of the Lord's Supper in the time of the administration of it?**

**Answer:** It is required of them that receive the sacrament of the Lord's Supper, that, during the time of the administration of it, with all holy reverence and attention they wait upon God in that ordinance,[1] diligently observe the sacramental elements and actions,[2] heedfully discern the Lord's body,[3] and affectionately meditate on his death and sufferings,[4] and thereby stir up themselves to a vigorous exercise of their graces;[5] in judging themselves,[6] and sorrowing for sin;[7] in earnest hungering and thirsting after Christ,[8] feeding on him by faith,[9] receiving of his fullness,[10] trusting in his merits,[11] rejoicing in his love,[12] giving thanks for his grace;[13] in renewing of their covenant with God,[14] and love to all the saints.[15]

[1] Lev. 10:3; Heb. 12:28; Psa. 5:7; 1 Cor. 11:17, 26-27. [2] Exod. 24:8 compared with Matt. 26:28. [3] 1 Cor. 11:29. [4] Luke 22:19. [5] 1 Cor. 11:26; 1 Cor. 10:3-5, 11, 14. [6] 1 Cor. 11:31. [7] Zech. 12:10. [8] Rev. 22:17. [9] John 6:35. [10] John 1:16. [11] Phil. 3:9. [12] Psa. 63:4-5; 2 Chron. 30:21; [13] Psa. 22:26. [14] Jer. 50:5; Psa. 50:5. [15] Acts 2:42.

**Question 175: What is the duty of Christians, after they have received the sacrament of the Lord's Supper?**

**Answer:** The duty of Christians, after they have received the sacrament of the Lord's Supper, is seriously to consider how they have behaved themselves therein, and with what success;[1] if they find quickening and comfort, to bless God for it,[2] beg the continuance of it,[3] watch against relapses,[4] fulfil their vows,[5] and encourage themselves to a frequent attendance on that ordinance:[6] but if they find no present benefit, more exactly to review their preparation to, and carriage at, the sacrament;[7] in both which, if they can approve themselves to God and their own consciences, they are to wait for the fruit of it in due time:[8] but, if they see they have failed in either, they are to be humbled,[9] and to attend upon it afterwards with more care and diligence.[10]

[1] Psa. 28:7; Psa. 85:8; 1 Cor. 11:17, 30-31. [2] 2 Chron. 30:21-23, 25-26; Acts 2:42, 46-47. [3] Psa. 36:10; Song of Sol. 3:4; 1 Chron. 29:18. [4] 1 Cor. 10:3-5, 12. [5] Psa. 50:14. [6] 1 Cor. 11:25-26; Acts 2:42, 46. [7] Song of Sol. 5:1-6; Eccles. 5:1-6. [8] Psa. 123:1-2; Psa. 42:5, 8; Psa. 43:3-5. [9] 2 Chron. 30:18-19; Isa. 1:16, 18. [10] 2 Cor. 7:11; 1 Chron. 15:12-14.

**Question 176: Wherein do the sacraments of baptism and the Lord's Supper agree?**

**Answer:** The sacraments of baptism and the Lord's Supper agree, in that the author of both is God;[1] the spiritual part of both is Christ and his benefits;[2] both are seals of the same covenant,[3] are to be dispensed by ministers of the gospel, and by none other;[4] and to be continued in the church of Christ until his second coming.[5]

[1] Matt. 28:19; 1 Cor. 11:23. [2] Rom. 6:3-4; 1 Cor. 10:16. [3] Rom. 4:11 compared with Col. 2:12; Matt. 26:27-28. [4] John 1:33; Matt. 28:19; 1 Cor. 11:23; 1 Cor. 4:1; Heb. 5:4. [5] Matt. 28:19-20; 1 Cor. 11:26.

### Question 177: Wherein do the sacraments of baptism and the Lord's Supper differ?

**Answer:** The sacraments of baptism and the Lord's Supper differ, in that baptism is to be administered but once, with water, to be a sign and seal of our regeneration and ingrafting into Christ,[1] and that even to infants;[2] whereas the Lord's Supper is to be administered often, in the elements of bread and wine, to represent and exhibit Christ as spiritual nourishment to the soul,[3] and to confirm our continuance and growth in him,[4] and that only to such as are of years and ability to examine themselves.[5]

[1] Matt. 3:11; Titus 3:5; Gal. 3:27. [2] Gen. 17:7, 9; Acts 2:38-39; 1 Cor. 7:14. [3] 1 Cor. 11:23-26. [4] 1 Cor. 10:16. [5] 1 Cor. 11:28-29.

### Question 178: What is prayer?

**Answer:** Prayer is an offering up of our desires unto God,[1] in the name of Christ,[2] by the help of his Spirit;[3] with confession of our sins,[4] and thankful acknowledgment of his mercies.[5]

[1] Psa. 62:8. [2] John 16:23. [3] Rom. 8:26. [4] Psa. 32:5-6; Dan. 9:4. [5] Phil. 4:6.

### Question 179: Are we to pray unto God only?

**Answer:** God only being able to search the hearts,[1] hear the requests,[2] pardon the sins,[3] and fulfil the desires of all;[4] and only to be believed in,[5] and worshipped with religious worship;[6] prayer, which is a special part thereof,[7] is to be made by all to him alone,[8] and to none other.[9]

[1] 1 Kings 8:39; Acts 1:24; Rom. 8:27. [2] Psa. 65:2. [3] Mic. 7:18. [4] Psa. 145:18-19. [5] Rom. 10:14. [6] Matt. 4:10. [7] 1 Cor. 1:2. [8] Psa. 50:15. [9] Rom. 10:14.

### Question 180: What is it to pray in the name of Christ?

**Answer:** To pray in the name of Christ is, in obedience to his command,

and in confidence on his promises, to ask mercy for his sake;[1] not by bare mentioning of his name,[2] but by drawing our encouragement to pray, and our boldness, strength, and hope of acceptance in prayer, from Christ and his mediation.[3]

[1] John 14:13-14; John 16:24; Dan. 9:17. [2] Matt. 7:21. [3] Heb. 4:14-16; 1 John 5:13-15.


## Question 181: Why are we to pray in the name of Christ?

**Answer:** The sinfulness of man, and his distance from God by reason thereof, being so great, as that we can have no access into his presence without a mediator;[1] and there being none in heaven or earth appointed to, or fit for, that glorious work but Christ alone,[2] we are to pray in no other name but his only.[3]

[1] John 14:6; Isa. 59:2; Eph. 3:12. [2] John 6:27; Heb. 7:25-27; 1 Tim. 2:5. [3] Col. 3:17; Heb. 13:15.


## Question 182: How doth the Spirit help us to pray?

**Answer:** We not knowing what to pray for as we ought, the Spirit helpeth our infirmities, by enabling us to understand both for whom, and what, and how prayer is to be made; and by working and quickening in our hearts (although not in all persons, nor at all times, in the same measure) those apprehensions, affections, and graces which are requisite for the right performance of that duty.[1]

[1] Rom. 8:26-27; Psa. 10:17; Zech. 12:10.


## Question 183: For whom are we to pray?

**Answer:** We are to pray for the whole church of Christ upon earth;[1] for magistrates,[2] and ministers;[3] for ourselves,[4] our brethren,[5] yea, our enemies;[6] and for all sorts of men living,[7] or that shall live hereafter;[8] but not for the dead,[9] nor for those that are known to have sinned the sin unto death.[10]

[1] Eph. 6:18; Psa. 28:9. [2] 1 Tim. 2:1-2. [3] Col. 4:3. [4] Gen. 32:11. [5] James 5:16. [6] Matt. 5:44. [7] 1 Tim. 2:1-2. [8] John 17:20; 2 Sam. 7:29. [9] 2 Sam. 12:21-23. [10] 1 John 5:16.


## Question 184: For what things are we to pray?

**Answer:** We are to pray for all things tending to the glory of God,[1] the welfare of the church,[2] our own[3] or others' good;[4] but not for anything that is unlawful.[5]

[1] Matt. 6:9. [2] Psa. 51:18; Psa. 122:6. [3] Matt. 7:11. [4] Psa. 125:4. [5] 1 John 5:14.

### Question 185: How are we to pray?

**Answer:** We are to pray with an awful apprehension of the majesty of God,[1] and deep sense of our own unworthiness,[2] necessities,[3] and sins;[4] with penitent,[5] thankful,[6] and enlarged hearts;[7] with understanding,[8] faith,[9] sincerity,[10] fervency,[11] love,[12] and perseverance,[13] waiting upon him,[14] with humble submission to his will.[15]

[1] Eccles. 5:1. [2] Gen. 18:27; Gen. 32:10. [3] Luke 15:17-19. [4] Luke 18:13-14. [5] Psa. 51:17. [6] Phil. 4:6. [7] 1 Sam. 1:15; 1 Sam. 2:1. [8] 1 Cor. 14:15. [9] Mark 11:24; James 1:6. [10] Psa. 145:18; Psa. 17:1. [11] James 5:16. [12] 1 Tim. 2:8. [13] Eph. 6:18. [14] Mic. 7:7. [15] Matt. 26:39.

### Question 186: What rule hath God given for our direction in the duty of prayer?

**Answer:** The whole word of God is of use to direct us in the duty of prayer;[1] but the special rule of direction is that form of prayer which our Saviour Christ taught his disciples, commonly called *The Lord's Prayer.*[2]

[1] 1 John 5:14. [2] Matt. 6:9-13; Luke 11:2-4.

### Question 187: How is the Lord's Prayer to be used?

**Answer:** The Lord's Prayer is not only for direction, as a pattern, according to which we are to make other prayers; but may also be used as a prayer, so that it be done with understanding, faith, reverence, and other graces necessary to the right performance of the duty of prayer.[1]

[1] Matt. 6:9 compared with Luke 11:2.

### Question 188: Of how many parts doth the Lord's Prayer consist?

**Answer:** The Lord's Prayer consists of three parts; a preface, petitions, and a conclusion.

### Question 189: What doth the preface of the Lord's Prayer teach us?

**Answer:** The preface of the Lord's Prayer (contained in these words, *Our Father which art in heaven*),[1] teacheth us, when we pray, to draw near to

God with confidence of his fatherly goodness, and our interest therein;[2] with reverence, and all other child-like dispositions,[3] heavenly affections,[4] and due apprehensions of his sovereign power, majesty, and gracious condescension:[5] as also, to pray with and for others.[6]

[1] Matt. 6:9. [2] Luke 11:13; Rom. 8:15. [3] Isa. 64:9. [4] Psa. 123:1; Lam. 3:41. [5] Isa. 63:15-16; Neh. 1:4-6. [6] Acts 12:5.

### Question 190: What do we pray for in the first petition?

**Answer:** In the first petition, (which is, *Hallowed by thy name*),[1] acknowledging the utter inability and indisposition that is in ourselves and all men to honour God aright,[2] we pray, that God would by his grace enable and incline us and others to know, to acknowledge, and highly to esteem him,[3] his titles,[4] attributes,[5] ordinances, word,[6] works, and whatsoever he is pleased to make himself known by;[7] and to glorify him in thought, word,[8] and deed:[9] that he would prevent and remove atheism,[10] ignorance,[11] idolatry,[12] profaneness,[13] and whatsoever is dishonourable to him;[14] and, by his over-ruling providence, direct and dispose of all things to his own glory.[15]

[1] Matt. 6:9. [2] 2 Cor. 3:5; Psa. 51:15. [3] Psa. 67:2-3. [4] Psa. 83:18. [5] Psa. 86:10-13, 15. [6] 2 Thess. 3:1; Psa. 147:19-20; Psa. 138:1-3; 2 Cor. 2:14-15. [7] Psa. 145; Psa. 8. [8] Psa. 103:1; Psa. 19:14. [9] Phil. 1:9, 11. [10] Psa. 67:1-4. [11] Eph. 1:17-18. [12] Psa. 97:7. [13] Psa. 74:18, 22-23. [14] 2 Kings 19:15-16. [15] 2 Chron. 20:6, 10-12; Psa. 83; Psa. 140:4, 8.

### Question 191: What do we pray for in the second petition?

**Answer:** In the second petition, (which is, *Thy kingdom come*),[1] acknowledging ourselves and all mankind to be by nature under the dominion of sin and Satan,[2] we pray, that the kingdom of sin and Satan may be destroyed,[3] the gospel propagated throughout the world,[4] the Jews called,[5] the fullness of the Gentiles brought in;[6] the church furnished with all gospel-officers and ordinances,[7] purged from corruption,[8] countenanced and maintained by the civil magistrate:[9] that the ordinances of Christ may be purely dispensed, and made effectual to the converting of those that are yet in their sins, and the confirming, comforting, and building up of those that are already converted:[10] that Christ would rule in our hearts here,[11] and hasten the time of his second coming, and our reigning with him forever:[12] and that he would be pleased so to exercise the kingdom of his power in all the world, as may best conduce to these ends.[13]

[1] Matt. 6:10. [2] Eph. 2:2-3. [3] Psa. 68:1, 18; Rev. 12:10-11. [4] 2 Thess. 3:1. [5] Rom. 10:1. [6] John 17:9, 20; Rom. 11:25-26; Psa. 67. [7] Matt. 9:38; 2 Thess. 3:1. [8] Mal. 1:11; Zeph. 3:9. [9] 1 Tim. 2:1-2. [10] Acts 4:29-30; Eph. 6:18-20; Rom. 15:29-30, 32; 2 Thess. 1:11; 2 Thess. 2:16-17. [11] Eph. 3:14-20. [12] Rev. 22:20. [13] Isa. 64:1-2; Rev. 4:8-11.

### Question 192: What do we pray for in the third petition?

**Answer:** In the third petition, (which is, *Thy will be done in earth as it is in heaven*),[1] acknowledging, that by nature we and all men are not only utterly unable and unwilling to know and do the will of God,[2] but prone to rebel against his word,[3] to repine and murmur against his providence,[4] and wholly inclined to do the will of the flesh, and of the devil:[5] we pray, that God would by his Spirit take away from ourselves and others all blindness,[6] weakness,[7] indisposedness,[8] and perverseness of heart;[9] and by his grace make us able and willing to know, do, and submit to his will in all things,[10] with the like humility,[11] cheerfulness,[12] faithfulness,[13] diligence,[14] zeal,[15] sincerity,[16] and constancy,[17] as the angels do in heaven.[18]

[1] Matt. 6:10. [2] Rom. 7:18; Job 21:14; 1 Cor. 2:14. [3] Rom. 8:7. [4] Exod. 17:7; Num. 14:2. [5] Eph. 2:2. [6] Eph. 1:17-18. [7] Eph. 3:16. [8] Matt. 26:40-41. [9] Jer. 31:18-19. [10] Psa. 119:1, 8, 35-36; Acts 21:14. [11] Mic. 6:8. [12] Psa. 100:2; Job 1:21; 2 Sam. 15:25-26. [13] Isa. 38:3. [14] Psa. 119:4. [15] Rom. 12:11. [16] Psa. 119:80. [17] Psa. 119:112. [18] Isa. 6:2-3; Psa. 103:20-21; Matt. 18:10.

### Question 193: What do we pray for in the fourth petition?

**Answer:** In the fourth petition, (which is, *Give us this day our daily bread*),[1] acknowledging, that in Adam, and by our own sin, we have forfeited our right to all the outward blessings of this life, and deserve to be wholly deprived of them by God, and to have them cursed to us in the use of them;[2] and that neither they of themselves are able to sustain us,[3] nor we to merit,[4] or by our own industry to procure them;[5] but prone to desire,[6] get,[7] and use them unlawfully:[8] we pray for ourselves and others, that both they and we, waiting upon the providence of God from day to day in the use of lawful means, may, of his free gift, and as to his fatherly wisdom shall seem best, enjoy a competent portion of them;[9] and have the same continued and blessed unto us in our holy and comfortable use of them,[10] and contentment in them;[11] and be kept from all things that are contrary to our temporal support and comfort.[12]

[1] Matt. 6:11. [2] Gen. 2:17; Gen. 3:17; Rom. 8:20-22; Jer. 5:25; Deut. 28:15-68.

³ Deut. 8:3. ⁴ Gen. 32:10. ⁵ Deut. 8:17-18. ⁶ Jer. 6:13; Mark 7:21-22. ⁷ Hos. 12:7.
⁸ James 4:3. ⁹ Gen. 43:12-14; Gen. 28:20; Eph. 4:28; 2 Thess. 3:11-12; Phil. 4:6.
¹⁰ 1 Tim. 4:3-5. ¹¹ 1 Tim. 6:6-8. ¹² Prov. 30:8-9.

### Question 194: What do we pray for in the fifth petition?

**Answer:** In the fifth petition, (which is, *Forgive us our debts, as we for-give our debtors*),[1] acknowledging, that we and all others are guilty both of original and actual sin, and thereby become debtors to the justice of God; and that neither we, nor any other creature, can make the least satisfaction for that debt:[2] we pray for ourselves and others, that God of his free grace would, through the obedience and satisfaction of Christ, apprehended and applied by faith, acquit us both from the guilt and punishment of sin,[3] accept us in his Beloved;[4] continue his favour and grace to us,[5] pardon our daily failings,[6] and fill us with peace and joy, in giving us daily more and more assurance of forgiveness;[7] which we are the rather emboldened to ask, and encouraged to expect, when we have this testimony in ourselves, that we from the heart forgive others their offences.[8]

¹ Matt. 6:12. ² Rom. 3:9-22; Matt. 18:24-25; Psa. 130:3-4. ³ Rom. 3:24-26; Heb. 9:22. ⁴ Eph. 1:6-7. ⁵ 2 Pet. 1:2. ⁶ Hos. 14:2; Jer. 14:7. ⁷ Rom. 15:13; Psa. 51:7-10, 12. ⁸ Luke 11:4; Matt. 6:14-15; Matt. 18:35.

### Question 195: What do we pray for in the sixth petition?

**Answer:** In the sixth petition, (which is, *And lead us not into temptation, but deliver us from evil*),[1] acknowledging, that the most wise, righteous, and gracious God, for divers holy and just ends, may so order things, that we may be assaulted, foiled, and for a time led captive by temptations;[2] that Satan,[3] the world,[4] and the flesh, are ready powerfully to draw us aside, and ensnare us;[5] and that we, even after the pardon of our sins, by reason of our corruption,[6] weakness, and want of watchfulness,[7] are not only subject to be tempted, and forward to expose ourselves unto temptations,[8] but also of ourselves unable and unwilling to resist them, to recover out of them, and to improve them;[9] and worthy to be left under the power of them:[10] we pray, that God would so over-rule the world and all in it,[11] subdue the flesh,[12] and restrain Satan,[13] order all things,[14] bestow and bless all means of grace,[15] and quicken us to watchfulness in the use of them, that we and all his people may by his providence be kept from being tempted to sin;[16] or, if tempted, that by his Spirit we may be powerfully supported and enabled to stand in the hour of temptation;[17] or when fallen, raised again and recovered out of it,[18] and have a sanctified use and improvement thereof:[19] that our sanctification and salvation may be perfected,[20] Satan trodden under our feet,[21] and we fully freed from sin, temptation, and all evil, for ever.[22]

[1] Matt. 6:13. [2] 2 Chron. 32:31. [3] 1 Chron. 21:1. [4] Luke 21:34; Mark 4:19. [5] James 1:14. [6] Gal. 5:17. [7] Matt. 26:41. [8] Matt. 26:69-72; Gal. 2:11-14; 2 Chron. 18:3 compared with 2 Chron. 19:2. [9] Rom. 7:23-24; 1 Chron. 21:1-4; 2 Chron. 16:7-10. [10] Psa. 81:11-12. [11] John 17:15. [12] Psa. 51:10; Psa. 119:133. [13] 2 Cor. 12:7-8. [14] 1 Cor. 10:12-13. [15] Heb. 13:20-21. [16] Matt. 26:41; Psa. 19:13. [17] Eph. 3:14-17; 1 Thess. 3:13; Jude 24. [18] Psa. 51:12. [19] 1 Pet. 5:8-10. [20] 2 Cor. 13:7, 9. [21] Rom. 16:20; Zech. 3:2; Luke 22:31-32. [22] John 17:15; 1 Thess. 5:23.

### Question 196: What doth the conclusion of the Lord's Prayer teach us?

**Answer:** The conclusion of the Lord's Prayer, (which is, *For thine is the kingdom, and the power, and the glory, for ever. Amen.*)[1] teacheth us to enforce our petitions with arguments,[2] which are to be taken, not from any worthiness in ourselves, or in any other creature, but from God;[3] and with our prayers to join praises,[4] ascribing to God alone eternal sovereignty, omnipotency, and glorious excellency;[5] in regard whereof, as he is able and willing to help us,[6] so we by faith are emboldened to plead with him that he would,[7] and quietly to rely upon him, that he will fulfil our requests.[8] And, to testify this our desire and assurance, we say, *Amen.*[9]

[1] Matt. 6:13. [2] Rom. 15:30. [3] Dan. 9:4, 7-9, 16-19. [4] Phil. 4:6. [5] 1 Chron. 29:10-13. [6] Eph. 3:20-21; Luke 11:13. [7] 2 Chron. 20:6, 11. [8] 2 Chron. 14:11. [9] 1 Cor. 14:16; Rev. 22:20-21.

**BANNER** *of* **TRUTH**

The Banner of Truth Trust originated in 1957 in London. The founders believed that much of the best literature of historic Christianity had been allowed to fall into oblivion and that, under God, its recovery could well lead not only to a strengthening of the church, but to true revival.

Interdenominational in vision, this publishing work is now international, and our lists include a number of contemporary authors, together with classics from the past. The translation of these books into many languages is encouraged.

A monthly magazine, *The Banner of Truth*, is also published, and further information about this, and all our other publications, may be found on our website, banneroftruth.org, or by contacting the offices below:

*Head Office:*
3 Murrayfield Road
Edinburgh
EH12 6EL
United Kingdom
Email: info@banneroftruth.co.uk

*North America Office:*
610 Alexander Spring Road
Carlisle, PA 17015
United States of America
Email: info@banneroftruth.org